A

The Gospel Truth!

By D. G. Miles McKee

Preface

It is hoped that those who come into possession of this book will be helped to grow in the gospel and will thus be better equipped to spread the good news. Part of the inspiration for this volume came from reading, 'God's Way of Peace' by Horatius Bonar and although this is neither a revision nor abridgment of Bonar's masterful work, Bonar's influence, one hopes, can be felt throughout the following pages small.

Introduction

Gandhi, the great hero of India, once said, "*If Christians would really live according to the teachings of Christ, as found in the Bible, all of India would be Christian today!*"

Many well-meaning Christians have since seized upon those words and have attempted, at times, to make the rest of us feel guilty about the many deficiencies in our Christian living. And do you know what? ... There's some truth in the things they say about our lifestyles. They're correct; our behaviour ought to make us stand out from the society around us. We ought to be more loving, generous and forgiving. The problem is, however, that we can preach as much as we like about Christian living, but if the gospel is not the centre of the message, the listeners will be left powerless to change. It is only a clear beholding of Christ's cross and righteousness that will effectually kill sin and cause us to grow in grace. The 18th century English preacher, John Berridge, confirmed this when he said that, in the days before he understood the gospel, he preached on morality so much that after several years there wasn't one moral person left in his parish!

But back to Gandhi! Gandhi was genuinely distressed by the racism and hypocrisy which he encountered in Christian churches! But was Gandhi correct in his analysis? Would India have become Christian if all the Christians had followed the teachings of Christ? No sir---not by a long shot!

Gandhi, like countless others fail to grasp that there is no such scripture that says, *"The gospel of good behaviour and a changed life is the power of God unto salvation."* Of course the gospel changes us, but the gospel which delivers nations is the gospel of Christ! The gospel is about Christ Jesus, not about our changed lives! It is the gospel of Christ that is the power of God unto salvation to those who believe. Our lives, no matter how spotless can never qualify as or rival this.

Someone once said,

"You're writing a gospel, a chapter each day...
By the deeds that you do, by the words that you say...
People read what you write, whether faithless or true
Say, what is the gospel according to you?"

Cute, but sheer nonsense! The gospel has already been written and written in blood---God's blood! The gospel is not about "the deeds that I do", but rather about the deeds that Christ has done! 'But' says someone, "Isn't it true that Christians are supposed to be loving?" Yes indeed that is true. Jesus said so in John 13:35 and John 15:12. But to assume that people will flock to become Christ's disciples because they see the love in the redeemed community is to invest these scriptures with more meaning than is intended. We are to love one another as Christ commanded, but our loving one another will not get people right before God. Just as no one is acquitted before God by having a changed life, so equally, no one is suddenly inspired to flee to God for mercy merely by observing our Christ-like life.

Yet, so much supposedly 'sound' preaching focuses on the inner experiences of change as though that was the paramount thing on the Father's mind! The thing of paramount importance to the Father, however, is the Son. It is His desire that in all things Christ would be pre-eminent (Colossians 1:18-19). The Father delights in Christ and so should we. He has glorified His Son and so should we!

Christ and His gospel is the key to Christian growth for the believer. As C.J. Mahaney eloquently says, *"If there's anything in life that we should be passionate about, it's the gospel. And I don't mean passionate only about sharing it with others. I mean passionate about thinking about it, dwelling on it, rejoicing in it, allowing it to color the way we look at the world. Only one thing can be of first importance to each of us. And only the gospel ought to have that place in our hearts."*

C J Mahaney: The Cross-Centered Life: Keeping the Gospel the Main Thing

To substitute the preaching of Christ crucified for a message about us is a travesty. However, by and large, subjective preaching has conquered many of our pulpits. And is it any wonder? In many evangelical circles nowadays, salvation is actually seen as the inward experience of new birth. Regeneration, in the thinking of many, has replaced Justification by grace through faith as the ground of acceptance before God. Rather than, by faith alone, resting on and embracing Christ alone, people are now being taught to look inward. Gandhi's words, therefore, resonate with many who now falsely believe that the power to get others saved lies within them, in the condition of their hearts and in their behaviour!

If all of India, or any country for that matter, is to come to Christ then the gospel of Christ needs to be restored to its rightful place.
Our churches and missionaries need to once more, become gospel driven! Since Christ's person, work and offices are the centre and heart of the gospel, they need to be proclaimed loudly and continually.

And that's the Gospel Truth!

Would you like to know whether or not you are gospel driven?

To find out, ask yourself these following questions.

With which are you absorbed? (Answer A or B)

1 (A) your personal righteousness or (B) the vicarious righteousness of Christ?

2 (A) the condition of your faith or (B) Christ's faithful obedience on your behalf?

3 (A) Your self-crucifixion or (B) His crucifixion?

4 (A) Your new life or (B) His sinless life?

5 (A) Your experience of Christ or (B) His experience for you?

6 (A) Your love for God or (B) His love for you?

7 (A) The depth of your personal surrender or (B) the depth of Christ's personal surrender?

8 (A) Your victorious life or (B) His victorious life?

9 (A) Your attainment or (B) His atonement?

10 (A) The work of the Spirit in you or (B) the work of Christ for you?

If you answered "B" in all 10 questions, you have a grasp of the gospel and better yet, the gospel has a grasp of you.

And that's the Gospel Truth!

Table of contents

Chapter 42: When Necessary Use Words...? Conclusion

Chapter 1

Saved by Someone Else

There are some church folk whom I've met who think that, simply by doing religious things, they can avoid divine displeasure and secure God's favour (Luke 18:10-12). It's sad to say but, we can all, at times, slip into that kind of thinking. We secretly hope that if we can just do enough for God we will somehow find forgiveness before we die? But this is a dangerous way of looking at things! Why? Because, by thinking in this manner, we are following a God of our own making! ... It's easy to do. At times, we can all be guilty of creating our own heavenward acceptance system. That's why we, as believers, need the gospel; it continually clears the poisonous, legalistic thinking out of our brains.

In the gospel, we don't end with acceptance before God, we begin with it! We commence our Christian life with full acceptance in Christ as we are embraced by God's perfect grace and acquittal (Romans 5:1). In the gospel, we are accepted by God, not because of our obedience, but because of

the obedience of someone else (Romans 5:19).
We are accepted, not because of our performance,
but accepted because of the performance of the
Lord Jesus in his life death, burial and resurrection.

Acceptance with God is one of the central benefits
of the gospel (Ephesians 1:6). Let's face it; there
can be no acceptable worship unless there are first
acceptable worshippers. But, notice how we
reverse things. When not instructed by the gospel,
we think that, by performing religious acts and
doing religious things, things like going to Church,
we can somehow find acceptance before God. This
is legalism, it's our default mode. However, the
gospel truth is that we must first be accepted and
then, and only then, are we qualified to acceptably
worship. Acceptable worship comes only from
accepted worshippers.

Man made religion presents forgiveness as the end
result of our efforts. But, again, this is not the
gospel. The gospel secures our forgiveness from
the very start. False religions are all essentially
alike---they are like the same cat with different
whiskers --- they teach that we should make
sincere efforts to secure God's forgiveness. But,

the truth is, our forgiveness has already been secured by the good works of the Lord Jesus. It is in Christ and in Christ alone that we have full divine favour and forgiveness! And it is by faith alone that we take hold of these wonderfully gracious gospel benefits.

Knowing this love of God, we can now enjoy being saved. We, as believers, are already fully loved, accepted and welcomed, by the Father, apart from our performance. This is good news! We don't have to earn God's smile of love for we already have it and have had it, in Christ, from before time. And in case you doubt this love, look at the Lamb of God, the Lord Jesus! It's in Him that we see love's full disclosure. See Him, hanging of on the cross, "Bearing shame and scoffing rude." It is in Jesus alone that we see the matchless grace of God towards us. When there was nothing we could do to save ourselves, He willingly became our substitute, and both lived and died in our place (see Isaiah 53).

We are saved by someone else; this is good news.

And that's the Gospel Truth!

Chapter 2

In Us and For Us---What's the Difference?

If ever we are to be established in the gospel, we must learn not to confuse the work of God for us with the work of God in us! The work of God for us is the work which God has accomplished, completed and perfected in the doing, dying and rising again of Christ (Romans 3:25-26). This magnificent work is the object of our faith. This work is finished.

The second great work is the work of God in us (Philippians 2:13)! This is the continuing, unfinished work of the Holy Spirit. It is sad to observe the endless mischief that has been unleashed on poorly taught Christians who confuse these two works. They fail to grasp that it is Christ's finished work for us which has secured our acquittal. They seem painfully unaware that no amount of the moving of the Spirit in our experience can improve upon Christ's experience on our behalf!

Looking at our experience and resting on it as our acceptance before the Father is a terrible mistake. In his excellent book, "The Doctrine of Justification, Professor James Buchanan tells us,

"There is, perhaps, no more subtle or plausible error, on the subject of Justification, than that which makes it to rest on the indwelling presence, and the gracious work, of the Holy Spirit in the heart."

Yet there are many who insist that they have had a thrilling experience when they were born again or filled with the Spirit. They tell us that because of these experiences they now know that they have been accepted by God. This is so very lethal! To put confidence and hope of heaven in the fact that something has happened within us is to rest on a quagmire. It is a fatal error.

Our righteousness is in Christ alone; this exalted Christ who, at this moment is applying the benefits of His redemption, is our resting place. This means that the work of the Spirit, vital though it is, can never be our righteousness.

By the Spirit, God gives us faith to look outside ourselves to the Saviour who is already enthroned in cosmic authority and majesty. Horatius Bonar says, and I paraphrase, "Faith, is the great identifier since it identifies us with the Lord Jesus Christ. Faith is the great grasper in that it grasps all that is in the Lord Jesus Christ! Faith is the great accepter in that it accepts the righteousness of Christ as the only hope of salvation."

 It is Christ and His work for us, done on our behalf, that saves us. Faith understands this. Concerning faith, let me again paraphrase Bonar: he says, *"Faith is really nothing but our consenting to be saved by someone else."* That's great!

As the Spirit works faith into our hearts we receive the glorious truth of the work done for us, apart from and outside of us 2000 years ago. He, the Spirit, generates faith under the hearing of the gospel and causes us to look to the all-sufficiency of Jesus and His finished work, outside of us, to save us. Faith causes us to see that God is just, and yet the justifier of all those who believe in Jesus (Romans 3:26). Faith sees that the penalty of sin has been taken away (1 John 8-10). Faith understands that the curse of the broken law has been removed (Galatians 3:13). Faith grasps that divine justice has been satisfied and that Satan has been defeated (Colossians 2:15, John 19:30).

It is no wonder then that gospel driven believers are thrilled with the Lord Jesus. We delight in Him for He alone is our hope and salvation. Faith has freed us from the bondage of having to look to our experience or our performance to find peace with God. Faith has taught us that all our hope is in Christ and His finished work, not in the work He is doing within us by His Spirit.

And that's the Gospel Truth!

Chapter 3

Sin on Him or in Him?

In this day and age when the gospel is under attack from all sides we must be aware of certain gospel foundations. For example, we must be clear about what Christ being *'made sin'* means. Was He made sin by *imputation* or by *impartation*? In other words, was Christ counted a sinner at the cross or was He physically made into one? The only answer which does justice to the Biblical evidence is that Christ was made sin by imputation and not by impartation.

Here's the problem, if Christ became wretchedly sinful in Himself then it follows that, because of the cross, we become perfectly righteousness in ourselves. Notice the following parallel, *"he hath made him to be sin for us, who knew no sin; that we might be made the righteousness of God in him (2 Corinthians 5:21)."* In the same way He was made sin, we are made righteous. In other words, at the cross, Christ was legally treated as if He were actually sinful in Himself although, in Himself, He remained righteous, pure and untainted.

Conversely, because of His finished work we are now legally treated as though we are perfectly righteous in ourselves---though, in actuality, we are not.

Christ was reckoned as sin that we might be reckoned as righteous. If, however, it was our sin 'in Him' that caused His damnation then it follows logically that His righteousness 'in us' is the cause of our acceptance ... a favoured doctrine of the Roman Communion. But sin was not in Him; it was reckoned (*imputed*) to Him and laid upon Him, but not infused into Him. His righteousness was in Him (Jeremiah 33:16) and we are treated as if we are righteous because the righteousness of Christ is reckoned to us (Isaiah 54:17).

This truth that sin was on Christ, but not in Him, is pictured in Abel's offering, the burnt offerings, the scapegoat and the transfer of sins to the innocent animals etc. Just as sins were imputed or reckoned to these animals, but not infused into them, so our sins were laid on Jesus, but not infused into Him (Isaiah 53:6).

This is not to say that Christ did not suffer and feel the effects of our sin. He took our curse and damnation to the fullest extent, yet in no way did He become a sinner. Only a sinless, perfect sacrifice could save us.

In Sunday School classes of the 1800s they taught the children that, at Calvary, there were three crosses and three dying men. One man was dying in sin (the unrepentant thief), another man was dying to sin (the repentant thief), but the man in the middle (Christ Jesus) was dying for sin. The children would then quote the following mantra, *"One man had sin both on him and in him. Another man had no sin on him but sin in him; Christ Jesus had sin on Him, but none in Him."* Those children were taught more than many of our dear adults today.

Our sins were not in Christ, they were on him and as such He received our awful penalty. His righteousness is, likewise, not created in us, but placed on us and as such we receive His marvellous reward. Our sin brought Jesus to the cross (Isaiah 53), but His righteousness will bring us to heaven (Philippians 3:8-9). Furthermore, when He suffered for sin, the shame was entirely ours. But, when we shall be glorified the glory shall be entirely His. When Christ died, there was nothing in Him worthy of death, yet death was his lot; similarly, there is nothing in us worthy of heaven, yet heaven is ours.

God executed His Son because our sin was on Him; likewise, God will glorify us because Christ's righteousness is on us. Death deserving sin was imputed to Christ and heaven deserving righteousness is imputed to us (Isaiah 53:11).

And that's the Gospel Truth!

Chapter 4

Don't Be Confused!

Here's another gospel foundation which we need to continually build into our thinking … although we are saved by faith, faith is not our saviour. There are those who erroneously teach that God looks at us and, if He sees faith, He declares us not guilty. This error, although taught by many, is a distorted, defiling of the gospel.

Believing that we are given eternal life because God looks and sees our faith, is to entirely miss the truth of the gospel. It is like the sick man who drives to the doctor, gets cured and then believes that his car healed him. Valuable as the car was in that it brought him to the doctor, it merely connected him with the healer. Likewise, faith connects us with our Great Physician, the Lord Jesus; faith brings us to Him, but faith, like the car, is neither our healer nor our Saviour!

In His masterpiece, 'The Everlasting Righteousness' Horatius Bonar writes,

"The bringer of the sacrifice into the tabernacle was to lay his hand upon the head of the sheep or the bullock; otherwise the offering would not have been accepted for him. But the laying on of his hand was not the same as the victim on which it was laid. The serpent-bitten Israelite was to look at the uplifted serpent of brass in order to be healed. But his looking was not the brazen serpent. We may say it was his looking that healed him, just as the Lord said, "Thy faith hath saved thee"; but this is figurative language. It was not his act of looking that healed him, but the object to which he looked."

Likewise, faith is not our righteousness: it merely knits us to the righteous One, and makes us partakers of His righteousness.

So, let's say it again, faith is not our saviour. It was not faith that was born as the representative of its people. It was not faith that fulfilled all righteousness; it was not faith that walked the weary road to Calvary; it was not faith that was executed in our place; it was not faith that bore our sins in its own body on the tree; it was not faith that poured out purchasing, redeeming blood. It was not faith that died and rose again for our sins … so let's be careful not confuse faith with its object, the Lord Jesus Christ (1 Timothy 3:16; Romans 5:19).

The object of our faith is Christ alone. He is our spiritual physician, and it is faith and faith alone which unites us to Him.

Continuing with the car analogy, let's say that we refuse to travel to Christ by faith and choose rather to capture His saving righteousness by taking church sacraments and performing good works. We would be like a man, travelling in the wrong direction, not this time in a car, but with the car strapped to his back. He's on the way to no towns and very few villages, ... and so are we if we look to religion or inward qualities to get us into right standing with God!

However, no church sacrament can save us for sacraments and ordinances cannot produce the perfect, completed righteousness required by God. The righteousness we need is the one which exists in Christ alone; it alone is the righteousness which presents us faultless before the throne of grace. But how do we make it ours? Is it by doing good, churchy things? No, the righteousness which saves us becomes ours by faith alone (Romans 4:22-25).

We do not obtain right standing before God because of our faith, but rather because of the doing, dying and rising again of our substitute and representative, Jesus Christ. His doing, dying and rising again is freely imputed to us and received by faith alone.

And that's the Gospel Truth!

Chapter 5

Needed, Perfection!

The righteousness which is needed to save us must be perfect. Indeed, God will accept nothing less than perfection (Hebrews 7:19). So either we have to be perfect in and of ourselves, or we need to be presented to God in the person of someone else who actually is perfect.

This is another reason why our faith can never be our saviour for our faith is not yet perfect. I don't know any believer who claims to have perfect faith. Doubtless our faith is growing; but, for that very reason, it cannot be considered perfect! It still has a long way to go! Here's the truth of the matter, since that which is imperfect cannot justify, an imperfect faith can in no way be counted as a perfect righteousness.

Faith cannot and will not rival the person of Christ for our justification. Saving faith, as it were, knows that Jesus is already perfect! He is *"the Lamb without blemish and without spot"* (1Peter 1:19). "He *did* no sin" (1 Peter 2:22). "He *knew* no sin (2

Corinthians 5:21), "*In Him* was no sin" (1 John 3:5). He was blameless in his actions, irreproachable in His motives, flawless in his thinking and sinlessly pure in all things. He is perfect!

One of the wonderful things about faith is that, although it is imperfect, it can still connect us with the perfection of Jesus. Faith looks at Jesus and sees His perfect love, perfect obedience, perfect faith, perfect worship, perfect prayer life, perfect grace, perfect truth, perfect righteousness and makes these things our own (1 Corinthians 1:30)! Faith sees that our sins have been purged perfectly. Faith sees that, at this very moment, Jesus is seated in cosmic majesty because His work of purging our sins is entirely finished and perfect (Hebrews 10:12,14).

Faith knows that our acceptance before God does not rest in any quality within us but in a quality outside of us—Christ Himself. His doing and dying is counted as ours. He and His work are perfect, and even though we are not, we stand complete in Him clothed with the very righteousness of heaven.

It is good news indeed that our faith does not need to be perfect in order to take hold of the perfect salvation which is in Christ alone. The truth is, if a perfect faith were required, then everyone would be lost. An imperfect faith is no shelter from the wrath of God. Don't look to your faith to be your saviour and don't worry about your faith being weak. Even a weak faith touches the perfect One, the Lord Jesus!

If we are looking to our faith and experience to find our security, we are on a fool's errand. Security is not found in our faith or in any experience, however genuine or thrilling. New Testament faith is faith in Christ alone. Our security is not in us, but in Him.

If a perfect faith were needed for our righteousness, the slightest flaw in our faith would be fatal. But God, in His glorious grace, has both demanded and provided us with a perfect righteousness, the Lord Jesus Himself (Romans 3:21-22). The Father is well pleased with the Lord Jesus and His work on our behalf, and neither asks for nor expects a perfect faith from us. This is good news for now we are free from having to endlessly stress over our level of faith.

All of us have crises of faith from time to time. In our worst moments, we may doubt our salvation and doubt our faith but that's a whole lot different than doubting the perfections of our Saviour. Doubt our salvation? ---Yes. Doubt our Saviour?-- Never! Even in our weakest moments the weakest of faith will connect us to the perfect righteousness of the Lord Jesus. We may be praying, "Lord, I believe; help thou mine unbelief" (Mark 9:24), but, even then, we are joined to the Perfect One!

And that's the Gospel Truth!

Chapter 6

Grace and Faith, His Part/My Part?

When I was younger, I thought that there were two parts to salvation, God's part and mine. I was saved by grace---that was God's part, through faith---that was my part. I had failed to read Ephesians 2:8 with anything other than my humanistic glasses and was, therefore, unconsciously determined that God should not have the entire glory for my salvation. But, through His kindness, the Lord eventually showed me the absolute absence of all saving goodness within me. My understanding increased, and faith graciously identified me with the complete saving right and ability of the Lord Jesus.

It is so crucial to learn that faith does not contribute to our salvation as there is no contribution needed. How, after all, can faith or anything else for that matter, improve on or add to an already perfect, finished work? Faith of course is necessary in that it accepts the finished, completed work which was accomplished 2000 years ago. Faith makes it our own. But, faith cannot augment or add to that work since that work is already done.

I had to learn that, in the gospel, there is no dividing or sharing the work between ourselves and the Lord Jesus. The entire work of redemption and reconciliation is His from first to last.

Here's where some people get confused in their understanding. They readily agree that they are saved by grace, but they don't realise that the concept of grace presupposes unworthiness. They don't seem to see that, if any of us were worthy of salvation, in any manner, salvation could not be by grace. They don't see that if salvation required any degree of worthiness on our part, it would then come to us as a reward.

Saving grace, however, is given exclusively to the unworthy and the undeserving. If we contribute anything to our salvation, no matter how small, grace ceases to be grace.

In a nutshell…We are saved entirely by grace or not at all. Grace is undeserved and unearned or not at all. We look for grace, clothed only in our unworthiness or not at all.

The scripture asks, "What do you have that you did not receive?" (See 1 Corinthians 4:7). What an excellent question! Faith is a free gift (Philippians 1:29) ... we received that! Repentance is a free gift (Acts 5:31) ... we received that! Righteousness is a free gift (Romans 5:17-18) ... we received that! God is the giver, we are the receivers. So let's ask it again, "What do you have that you didn't receive?" The answer is NOTHING! It delights the Father to save us by His free and extravagant grace from beginning to end. Boasting is, therefore, excluded (Romans 3:27). If we have received grace, it is not because we gave anything to deserve it --- and that includes faith (John 6:65)!

If we believe that faith is our part and not God's, then we have made ourselves co-providers of salvation. But this cannot be possible, for the scripture is abundantly clear that we are saved by grace alone.

We read in Psalms 115:1, "Not unto us, O LORD, not unto us, but unto thy name give glory, for thy mercy, and for thy truth's sake." Salvation by grace alone honours that verse! Faith will cause us to see the absurdity of trying to compete with God and will cause us to receive freely and willingly His gracious salvation. Faith identifies us with His doing and dying as if it were our very own.

Salvation is the gift of God (Ephesians 2:8). If we were to try to add our puny efforts to Christ's already finished salvation, it would be like Abel trying to add a daisy to his already acceptable offering of the substitute Lamb.

And that's the Gospel Truth!

Chapter 7

Truths that Faith Sees

Since repetition is the price of learning, let's say it again, we are saved by faith alone, but faith is not our saviour. Christ alone has that honour. Faith sees and grasps this. However, this is not the only truth that faith comprehends. For example, faith sees that Christ, in His perfect righteousness, lived as our substitute. Faith sees him unswervingly obeying His Father in our place. We could not keep God's requirements, but faith sees that Christ kept them perfectly on our behalf. As gospel driven believers, we know that we have never flawlessly obeyed God. In fact, when we see the intense purity of God's will and the extent of our matching impurity, faith sees that Christ's perfect obedience, in His doing and dying, is our only hope. In short, faith sees that what Jesus did, He did as if He were us----- He that believeth on him is not condemned (John 3:18).

As gospel believers, we must keep hammering home, to ourselves, the truth that, in this matter of salvation, we are not called to have faith about anything that is in us, even that which is worked into us by the Holy Spirit. But why not? It's simple! The faith that takes a hold of salvation looks outside of us to the risen, exalted Christ. Faith sees that He has taken our curse (Galatians 3:13). Faith also sees Him as the man who took our sorrows and was acquainted with our grief (Isaiah 53:3). Faith sees Him nailed to the cross, pouring out His blood for us. Faith agrees that by one offering, at the cross, Jesus perfected us forever (Hebrews 10:14)! Faith grasps that the Father will never find any blemish in Christ's perfect righteousness. Faith sees Christ now raised from the dead, ascended to heaven, and interceding for us. This is what it is to believe!

Since Christ was both condemned and separated from the Father in our stead, faith sees that, in Christ, there is neither condemnation nor separation from the Father (Romans 8:1, Romans 8:38-39). Faith further sees that the absence of condemnation and separation does not depend on our walk before God. Faith sees that it all depends on Christ's performance in His doing, dying and rising again. Under the law, we were both condemned and separated, but now, in Christ, both condemnation and separation from the Father have been done away.

At the cross, Christ was both condemned by and separated from the Father in our place. Faith sees this and enables us to now live our lives, not running away from God, but, rather, running straight to His embrace.

At a religious gathering some time ago, a woman stood and testified about her supposed salvation saying, "I thank God I'm saved; yes indeed, I'm saved up to the present date!" .... Neither faith, nor the Word, caused her to conclude such nonsense. What a lamentable way to live one's life! The poor soul had, evidently, no clue about the gospel. Would, for her sake, she had been taught by a gospel preacher like Spurgeon who said, concerning the impossibility of a justified person ever being condemned,

"Oh, for an overpowering faith that shall get the victory over doubts and fears, and make us enjoy the liberty with which Christ makes men free! You that believe in Christ, go to your beds this night and say, "If I die in my bed, I cannot be condemned!" Should you wake the next morning, go into the world and say, "I am not condemned!"

When the devil howls at you, tell him, "You may accuse, but I am not condemned!" And if sometimes your sins rise, say, "I know you, but you are all gone forever. I am not condemned!"

And that's the Gospel Truth!

Chapter 8

Beware of Wayward Teachers

The ministry of the Holy Spirit will never lead us away from the cross; it led us there in the beginning and will continue to do so until we see Jesus face to face (1 Corinthians 13:12). At no time in the believer's life do we cease to need the gospel.

However, some wayward teachers in this day and age suggest that we should go beyond the cross and leave it behind. (2 Peter 2:17-22). "The cross," they say "has done all it can do for us." They declare, *"It is, of course, right and correct to come under the shadow of the cross in the beginning of our Christian lives, but now,"* they insist, *"we need to move on to deeper things."* They maintain that to continue in the gospel of the crucified Christ is to remain but an immature, spiritual baby (2 Peter 2:18).

But, what is the cross? It is not a literal piece of wood from antiquity; rather, it is the central issue with God. The cross has been planned from eternity (Revelation 13:8), and, as such, we dare not remove it from being our core doctrine and delight. To leave the cross would be to leave the eternal purpose and counsel of God. To leave Christ Crucified as the core of our thinking would be to turn our back on the Lamb that was slain (Philippians 3:18). Yet, this is exactly what we do when we follow these 'modern men', these apostles of the 'New Thing that God is Speaking Now.' If we follow them, we replace Christ Jesus with novelties and fads which masquerade themselves as Christian truth.

"But, Christ crucified is only for beginners and we must move on from it," they insist. They, however, mistakenly assume that the preaching of Christ crucified means that we endlessly talk about the crown of thorns and the nails! No! It's bigger than that. The doing, dying and rising of the Lord Jesus is a comprehensive event which cannot be divided. We cannot, for example, separate Christ's sinless life from the cross--- they are vitally connected; one establishes the other. Furthermore, no part of this event, this gospel, shall ever become redundant or obsolete.

Concerning this truth, Horatius Bonar says,

"I am always at the manger, and yet I know that mere incarnation cannot save; always at Gethsemane, and yet I believe that its agony was not the finished work; always at the cross, with my face toward it and my eye on the crucified One, and yet I am persuaded that the sacrifice there was completed once for all; always looking into the grave, though I rejoice that it is empty and that "He is not here, but is risen"; always resting (with the angel) on the stone that was rolled away, and handling the grave-clothes, and realizing a risen Christ, no indeed, an ascended and interceding Lord; yet on no pretext whatever leaving any part of my Lord's life or death behind me, but unceasingly keeping up my connection with Him, as born, living, dying, buried, and rising again, and drawing out from each part some new blessing every day and hour."

There is no leaving of the gospel. The Holy Spirit keeps unfolding it in deeper and deeper ways. Beware, therefore, of preachers who are not centred on Christ crucified. In much the same way that a blind hog gets the occasional acorn, they can occasionally say helpful things, but the gospel is not the driving force of their preaching. Avoid them; they have no message. Although, their sermons are well packaged and smoothly delivered, they lack New Testament authentication since they are not centred in Christ Crucified. They will mention Christ, but, even then, it is usually "Christ in you" who gets central billing. They have no passion for the person and the objective, finished work of Christ. In their preaching, Christ will always take second place to the believer. The believers needs will be central to their message, and if we have no needs, they will be kind enough to contrive some for us.

It is intriguing to note that, in scripture, we read of true and false prophets, wise and foolish virgins, faithful and unfaithful stewards, true and false apostles, but one thing we never read of is true and false sheep. Sheep are sheep, called by God (Isaiah 42:6), held by God (Isaiah 41:10), prayed for by God (Hebrews 7:25) and sealed by God (Ephesians 4:30). And here's a distinguishing mark of the sheep, ----- they will not follow a stranger (John 10:5). They love their crucified and exalted shepherd. They will not fall prey to the wayward teacher who would lead them away from their Master.

And that's the Gospel Truth!

Chapter 9

Cancelling the Simplicity of the Cross

2 Corinthians 11:3 But I fear, lest by any means, as the serpent beguiled Eve through his subtlety, so your minds should be corrupted from the simplicity that is in Christ.

False teachers will always try to take us away from Christ Crucified. They offer formulas for successful Christian lives, but, although they tip their hats to Jesus, He is neither the centre nor the circumference of their message. *"If you do this"* they boast, *"then God will do thus and so for you." "Do and you'll get"* is their theme. But this is legalism 'pure and undefiled!' Gospel faith differs from this, in fact it's quite the opposite. Faith, real faith, will cause us to give up our exhausting and useless efforts to do or feel something good in order to coax God to love and bless us (Ephesians 2:8).

Unfortunately, we often stray from the gospel and feel that we need to make an extra special effort at godliness so that we can squeeze more acceptance from our Heavenly Father. We sometimes think that, if only we could spend more time in Bible reading, prayer and witnessing, then the Father would really count us as special. But to think this way is the very opposite of faith. It is actually unbelief. True faith always rests upon Christ alone to gain us full approval, acceptance and blessing before God.

Then, there's the religionist. Like the false teacher, the non-gospel, religious, self-satisfied man always tries to get away from Christ crucified. But, before we condemn and judge him, we'd better take a good hard look at ourselves. Stupid as it may seem, we often trust in our own performance more than in Christ's performance on our behalf (Galatians 6:3).

Furthermore, we would rather trust our own experience than that of Christ's experience for us. In doing so, we leave the gospel and fall headlong into works religion (Galatians 5:4). Remember this; the religious person doesn't mind adding the cross to their belief system. The cross becomes, as it were, one of their many collectable trinkets. But in making the cross something additional, he cancels its simplicity and reduces it to nothing. The cross, for him, is just something that he adds to, but the truth is, to add any kind of plus to the cross makes it nonplussed.

The truth is this; the cross saves completely or not at all. We can never, therefore, divide the work of salvation between ourselves and Christ. It is not our performance plus Christ's doing, dying and rising from the grave which gives favour with God and saves (Galatians 2:21). Faith grasps that Christ alone saves. Faith adds nothing to the cross for faith sees the fullness and sufficiency of the accomplished work and brings us to rest on Christ alone (2 Corinthians 3:4-5). To paraphrase Horatius Bonar, "We do not come to Calvary to add anything, we come by faith to see and hear something. At Calvary, faith sees the glorious truth that all things have already been sufficiently and completely accomplished and it also hears the 'It is Finished' of Christ Jesus the Sin-bearer (John 19:30). Faith, having caused us to see and hear, then causes us to say a hearty Amen."

Chapter 10

What Truths are we to Believe for Justification?

There are numerous, wonderful truths taught in the Bible, but which of them do we primarily need to believe to enjoy acceptance before God? Take the Second Coming of the Lord, for example, (1 Thessalonians 4:16-18): that Christ will one day return to this earth in great glory and majesty is an excellent truth. In fact, if someone claimed they were a believer, but rejected this truth we would probably question their salvation (1 John 3:3). Yet we are not in any sense acquitted before God by believing in the Second Coming of our Lord.

Faith also looks at the resurrection and sees in it the evidence that Christ satisfied the justice of God. Romans 4:25 tells us that He, "...*was raised again for our justification.'* Faith sees that the resurrection, therefore, was the visible pledge of a justification already accomplished. Resurrection is a vital, indispensable gospel truth and indeed there is no gospel without it. In spite of this, however, although the resurrection is the proof of our justification, it is not the ground of our justification.

We believe that Christ ascended into heaven (Ephesians 4:10) and sat down at the right hand of the majesty on high (Hebrews 10:12), but excellent as this truth is we are not declared "not guilty" by believing it.

We believe that the Holy Spirit has been sent to earth as Christ's substitute (John 14:16-20) and that He is actively calling out a bride for the wonderful Son of God, yet believing these things does not produce right standing before the thrice-holy God.

So what then is the belief we need to have in order to be saved? What we need is faith in the God/Man who was crucified. It is not merely enough to assent to the fact that He died; we must be possessed by a faith in Him. What we need is a faith that Christ, the man who is God, died as our substitute, our sin offering and in doing so, He removed the wrath of the all-holy God. But more than that, the faith that justifies grasps also that Christ is now our only righteousness (Romans 1:16-17). Faith sees that no other righteousness than Christ's is necessary for acceptance in heaven and that no other righteousness is either requested or required!

Faith will always bring us back to the Christ of cross as the ground and basis of our justification. He alone is our right standing before God. Out of Him flows every and all gospel benefit.

And that's the Gospel Truth!

Chapter 11

God's Verdict--It's Not Pretty!

"God knows us. He knows what we are, but He also knows what He meant us to be, and there's a vast difference!"
Horatius Bonar.

Consider this, since God is love (1 John 4:8), we can be assured that He is too loving to say anything needlessly harsh about us; but, since God is the God of truth (Deuteronomy 32:4), we can also be sure that, when He is describing us, He isn't telling us any lies!

So what does the God of Truth say about us? Now this may surprise you, He says that, in and of ourselves, we are entirely rotten (Isaiah 1:6)! This is not God being harsh --- He's too wonderfully kind to be harsh --- these are just the facts as God sees them. God looks at us and says that we are all ruined. OK those are not His actual words, but here's what He solemnly says word for word, "There is none righteous, no, not one," "there is none that does good" "there is none that seeks after God" (Romans 3:10 and following verses).

God loves us enough to be honest with us! In love, He declared man to be a lost stray (Psalm 58:3); a rebel (Hosea 7:14) and a hater of God (Matthew 6:24; Romans 1:30)." Man is neither an occasional nor partial sinner, but recklessly sins with heart and soul! If it were not for grace, those of us who are saved, would perish. How quickly we forget the pit from which we have been dug (Psalm 40:2)! According to God, man is so lost that there is nothing he can do to compensate for his lostness. He, by nature, is against God, spiritually dead (Ephesians 2:1) and already condemned (John 3:18). Man's condition is so lost that, unless Christ intervenes, he will perish eternally. Man is under "the curse of the law" (Daniel 9:11); and no, it is not a rare person who has fallen, but the entire race! In Adam, all have sinned, and, in Adam, all have died (Romans 5:12); all have gone astray (Isaiah 53:6) and all have come short of the glory of God (Romans 3:23).

This is dreadful news, but people deceive themselves into denying this distressing report. In their deception they insist that they are good enough for heaven (Luke 18:11)) and, in doing so, they enter into an un-winnable debate with God, displaying grave disregard and disagreement with Him. But no matter, in spite of man's opinions on the subject, God still says all are guilty and worthy of death and hell. God has made it clear, "*He that believeth not God, hath made him a liar; because he believeth not the record which God gave of his Son*" (1 John 5:10). The unsaved man refuses to worship and love God with all His strength, but even if he tried to (which he won't) he is incapable of doing so. He demonstrates, therefore, that he is indeed thoroughly guilty. God's verdict of man, therefore, to any rightly thinking person, is vindicated.

Not only does the unsaved man not love God with all his heart, he has no love for Him whatsoever. He loves His own will and purposes rather than God's. He will not submit to the One who is sustaining his life and lending Him breath.

It is pointless for man to try to argue the point of his own goodness or to plead "not guilty," unless he can show that he has always loved God with everything. If he can truly say this, he is in decent shape, he has never sinned and doesn't need acquittal through the shed blood of the Lord Jesus. He has no need for the gospel, the blood and the Saviour. But, if he cannot say that he has loved God with all, "his mouth is stopped," and he is "guilty before God" (Romans 3:19).

And that's the Gospel Truth!

Chapter 12

The Great Sin of the Religious, Self-Centred Man

The great sin of the self-righteous, self-centred man is not his pride; it is his unbelief. In His unbelief, he refuses to rest on the Father's gift of the Son (John 3:18; 1 John 5:10; 1 Corinthians 16:22). This is his most outrageous crime, a crime that carries with it a more concentrated condemnation than all his other sins combined.

Jesus taught, "When he (the Spirit) is come he will reprove the world of sin, and of righteousness, and of judgment --- because they believe not on me" (John 16:8-9). Notice how the Master says that the Spirit will convince the world of sin because they do not keep the Ten Commandments." Woops! Did I just say that? It must have been me for it absolutely was not the teaching of the Master.

According to Jesus, the first sin that the Holy Spirit convicts us of is, not that we are lawbreakers, but that we do not believe on Him. That is not to say that we are not lawbreakers. In fact, the law commands us to love the Lord with all that is within us and this we fail to do by not resting and abiding in the Lord Jesus. The Spirit's priority, therefore, is to reprove the world of the great sin of not resting on Christ alone. In other words, the essence of sin is not what we do but what we believe.

Here are the facts;

Not trusting in and resting on the Lord Jesus is the chief sin and root of all lawlessness. A lawless man is a man who is not resting on Christ alone.
A lawless man may talk a good talk and attend church meetings, but if he is not trusting on Christ alone, he is a rebel against heaven.

Out of this sin of rebellious unbelief flow all his other sins. Immorality is a sin rooted in unbelief. The reason people commit various acts of evil, adultery, murder and theft etc. is ultimately because they do not believe. A man who continuously lives in wilful sin such as adultery or fornication may claim to be a Christian, but he is wilful rebel.

The Holy Spirit also reproves of righteousness. He literally brings to light the uselessness of the world's righteousness. Notice, it's not unrighteousness that the Holy Spirit exposes (in John 16:8-9), but righteousness. The worldly, religious man thinks that he is righteous, but God strongly disagrees with Him (Romans 3:10 ff). Nowhere is this more clearly seen than at the cross. It was self-righteous, unbelieving, upstanding men who murdered the Lord Jesus. In their deceived and deluded minds, they thought they were acting righteously. In their self-righteous estimation, they were convinced that Jesus was wrong about both His doctrine and His identity. But after Jesus rose from the dead and ascended, the Spirit was sent to declare otherwise. In the light of the cross, self-satisfied, religious, prideful man was shown to be guilty. The cross, therefore, is God's settled verdict on the awful, sinful mass of filth that constituted man's righteousness (Isaiah 64:6). If ever the self-righteous are to be saved, the Spirit of God must show them that they need an entirely new righteousness---the righteousness of Christ Himself.

According to Jesus, the Holy Spirit also convinces the world of judgment ... not of their future judgment although, of course, that is coming to all Christ rejecters, but of judgment, "because the prince of this world has been judged" (John 16:11). At the cross, Satan's grip over us was destroyed. Satan has been judged, and all who believe in Christ Jesus are now free from his bondage. This is good news.

We are saved not only by grace but by power. May the Lord cause us to see how worthy of condemnation, bondage and ruin we are. May He enable us to be thrilled by His lavish, powerful grace (Luke 7:47b). Grace means that God has loved us for no other reason than that He has loved us! He who is all purity has loved us at our impure worst. Our guilt was met by His justice. Our well-earned wrath was intercepted by the Lord Jesus who rescued, ransomed, redeemed and reconciled us. That's grace!

And that's the Gospel Truth!

Chapter 13

Approaching God

No matter how many religious things we do, whether it's praying, giving or abstaining from worldliness, we cannot find, in any of them, qualifications by which we can approach the Father. Religious activity provides no resting place in which to discover the smile of God.

If sin were a simple thing like a disease, then perhaps religious observances might be useful in mending the gulf between us and the Almighty. But sin is much worse than any disease. The unsaved sinner is not merely 'sin-sick', he is 'sin-dead' (Ephesians 2:1). Worse still, he is under the righteous condemnation of inflexible justice (John 3:18). God, the unchangeable judge, has an unalterable hatred of sin and has warned about His coming wrath against the unsaved sinner (Matthew 23:33).

Unbelieving, self-righteous, religious people make the grave mistake of trying to present their character to God as the basis of approaching Him. Approaching God, however, has nothing whatsoever to do with our character. God says that our goodness, as a qualification, is an illusion and that there is no goodness in us qualifying or recommending us for His acceptance (Job 15:14-16). Ouch!

Unfortunately, there are many professing believers who think that, if they tell others about Jesus, study the Bible and are extremely earnest, then they are qualified to find a welcome from the Father. But, this makes zero sense! They started out with grace and are now trying to approach God through their performance (works)! Perhaps, their problem is even more severe. Maybe they didn't even start their "Christian life" with grace at all. Perhaps they began with works, the work of doing something---something like asking Jesus into their heart to get saved. What a treacherous foundation this has become for many. It's easy, therefore, for such a person to think that there is something he must continue to do to earn the welcome of God.

So let's start at the beginning and ask, "How does a guilty sinner approach God in the first place?" "Well, we pray," says someone. That's fair enough, but how can we actually approach God? After all, His explicit testimony against all of us is, "You are unfit to approach me in your own merit" (Psalm 53:2-3). To imagine that we can pray ourselves out of unfitness and into spiritual suitability is ridiculous. Unbeliever and believer alike must learn that our religious efforts can never be the basis of our approach to God. No amount of praying, working or feeling can satisfy the righteousness of God, or open the door to the presence of the Holy One.

So then, "How does a sinful man approach God and find acceptance before Him?" (Job 25:4). No appeal can be made to God based on our personal character, goodness, or religious performances (Romans 3:10 and following verses makes that clear). In that case, since God is not sufficiently impressed with our puny efforts, or with us, what then are we to do?

The good news is that we are not left to work this matter out for ourselves for God has already done something about this problem. He has already resolved the dilemma of how to approach Him. In fact, it was settled 2000 years ago in the doing, dying and rising again of Christ. This is why Jesus claimed to be the Way to the Father and the Door into heaven (John 10:9). And this is why we read that we have "boldness to enter into the holiest by the blood of Jesus," (Hebrews 10:19).

It only remains for us, by faith alone, to continuously receive what He has done. It is on the basis of Christ and His shed blood that we have our first and continual welcome in Heaven (Hebrews 10:22, Ephesians 3:12).

Wherewith shall we approach the Lord,
And bow before his Throne?
By trusting in His faithful word,
And pleading Christ alone.

The blood, the righteousness and love
Of Jesus we will plead
He lives within the veil above,
For us to intercede"

To approach God, we come to Him as needy and broken, dependent entirely on the person, work, name and grace of Christ Jesus our Saviour, Surety, Shepherd and Substitute.

And that's the Gospel Truth!

Chapter 14

Continual Acceptance Before God

As believers, one of the difficulties we encounter in the Christian life is that, if we are not continually bathed in the gospel, we quietly and almost imperceptibly begin to look for qualities within ourselves as being the ground and basis of our acceptance before God. But this is deception. Our exclusive appeal for continued acceptance before God is found in Christ alone!

We may be in Christian service and ministry, but we are not accepted because of our work for the Lord. Nor are we accepted because of the quantity of our prayers or the greatness of our faith. It is so liberating to remember that the only acceptance we have before God is Christ Himself! We are, "found in Him"(Philippians 3:9). This must mean that our own "self" has disappeared and instead, in the Father's eyes, there is Christ, the beloved Son in whom He is well pleased (Matthew 3:17).

Horatius Bonar observed, "Found in ourselves, there was nothing but wrath; found in Him there is nothing but favour." We are hidden in Christ (Colossians 3:3): we are complete in Him (Colossians 2:10). He is our continual acceptance before God.

As we grow in the grace, we recognise that although we are, within ourselves, unworthy of the Father's acceptance, we are actually accepted beyond measure. Also, gospel grace teaches us that we are totally loved in spite of being, in ourselves, totally unlovable. Gospel grace further informs us that we are totally accepted in spite of being, in ourselves, totally unacceptable.

Because we are in Christ, we no longer put confidence in the flesh (Philippians 3:3). Because we are in Christ, we are liberated from the search for acceptance with God through resolutions and vows to increase our dedication. The true believer knows that, in him, that is in his flesh, there dwells no good thing (Romans 7:18). He knows that compared to God, everything within Him is vileness and sin. The truth is, if man had the power to save Himself, he would not have the desire to do so; and if He had the desire to save himself, he would not have the power to do so. Apart from grace, he is ruined.

This is why the Holy Spirit always fixes our eyes on Christ (John 16:14). He never turns our eye in on our performance as a means of gaining confidence. He never leads us to get encouragement by looking at our own character or performance. No! The way by which the Spirit gives us confidence is to continually glorify and magnify the perfections of Lord Jesus Christ in our sight.

Are you living with something less than full assurance of your acceptance before the Father? Christ has died, Christ has risen and is even now seated in cosmic authority making intercession for you (Romans 8:34). Has unbelief caused you to doubt the abilities and will of your Saviour to save you? Do you doubt the truth of God's testimony? Do you honestly believe that the Rock of Ages is going to crumble?

John Bunyan said,

"Christ is all and in all" (Colossians 3:11). He who knows this knows what fully satisfies and cheers. He who knows this best has the deepest and truest peace: for he has learned the secret of being always a sinner, yet always righteous; always incomplete, yet always complete; always empty, and yet always full; always poor, and yet always rich."

For continued acceptance before God and a present, joyful assurance of salvation, we need Christ and His finished work plus nothing.

And that's the Gospel Truth!

Chapter 15

The Saviour, not a Helper

Though He was above the law, Christ took His place under the law to save us (Galatians 4: 4). He lived a sinless life, then, on the cross, endured the awful penalties of the law. Not only did He redeem us from the curse of the law (Galatians 3:13), He also fulfilled the law, for righteousness, to every one that believes (Romans 10:4). He took our beating so that we would have His blessings without barter.

We must always remember that Christ, when it comes to salvation, is not a helper, He is the Saviour! By this, I mean that He did not come to help us to save ourselves by keeping a more relaxed and toned down law. No! The gospel truth is that faith in Christ is not a means of setting aside the inflexible standard of the law. To the contrary, faith in Christ is, in reality, the only method of successfully meeting the law's demands. Faith in Christ Jesus is an acknowledgement that we are guilty before the law and incapable of mustering, within ourselves, a sufficient obedience to meet its requirements. At the same time, faith in Christ, also acknowledges that the Lord Jesus has kept the unadulterated law in our place. Faith recognises that the Lord Christ came to fulfil the Law on our behalf! He is the Saviour, not a helper!

The cross was the satisfaction rendered for all the unfulfilled and violated demands of the divine majesty. That which God's law righteously required, God graciously provided in the doing and dying of the Lord Jesus Christ. Christ's substitutionary life and death satisfied the just demands of the violated law. This is good news! All who believe and rely on the Christ of God have, by righteous grace, been credited with the entirety of His accomplishments. As a result, all believers are now seen as perfect law keepers in the eyes of the Father.

Consider how the Father dealt with Jesus on the cross. Christ was the eternal Word made flesh. He was the righteousness of God, yet He was, "numbered with the transgressors"(Isaiah 53:12). Justice dealt with Him, not according to what He was in Himself, but treated Him as though He were us.

At the cross, our sins were imputed (legally reckoned) to Him.
At the cross, His righteousness was imputed (legally reckoned) to us.

In Romans 4, the marvellous little word logizomai (impute, reckon, count) appears eleven times. Paul illustrated this powerful word when he wrote to his friend about Onesimus, the runaway slave. He says in verse 18 of the letter to Philemon that if Onesimus owes anything, or if he's wronged you in any way, put that to my account. This is imputation. Our debts are put into Christ's account, and Christ's righteousness is put into ours.

There was a man who was once preaching the gospel to some English fishermen. His subject was justification by free grace and he was trying to make Christ's work on the cross both clear and plain. He finally asked the men the question, "Now will one of you tell me in your own words what the Lord Jesus Christ did on the cross?" One old fisherman who had been deeply moved by the message, with some tears in his eyes looked up at the preacher and answered, "He swapped with me." What a great answer! This man had grasped the truth of the penal, substitutionary sacrifice of the Lord Jesus Christ. Our salvation is only in him. He is the Saviour, not a helper.

And that's the Gospel Truth!

Chapter 16

Christ Will Do!

The only reason it is safe for us to approach God and right for God to receive us is because of something that has been accomplished entirely outside of ourselves. Apart from the doing, dying and rising again of Christ, we have no hope (Romans 3:10 and following verses). But here's how ridiculous things are; condemned men whose best efforts are rejected by heaven, try to use religious works to impress God. In doing so, they reject that Christ alone is enough to mend the separation between them and the Almighty and thus they reject God's only solution to their dilemma. The unsaved will try anything and everything other than resting on Christ alone for their entire salvation.

Horatius Bonar in his book, God's Way of Peace, tells the story of a man, troubled by his sense of separation from God, who thought that, if he could just pray hard enough, he could mend the breach between himself and the Father. The Lord, he felt, would be impressed enough by his prayers to accept him. Not much progress was being made, so he doubled the amount of his devotions, saying to himself, "*Surely if I try harder, God will take notice and will give me peace.*" But no peace came. He then set up family worship in his home, reasoning, "*Now the Lord is bound to take notice of me and consider my efforts.*" But there was still an immense awareness of his separation. Eventually, he decided to have a prayer meeting in his house and set a particular night aside; invited his neighbours; and prepared himself for conducting the meeting, by writing a prayer and learning it off by heart. As he finished learning it, he threw it down on the table saying, "*Surely that will do, God will give me peace now.*" In that moment, a still small voice seemed to speak to him saying, "*No, that will not do; but Christ will do.*" Immediately, the scales fell from his eyes, and he saw that Christ had done enough in His doing dying and rising again. He saw that his efforts to impress God were redundant to the uttermost.

Instantly, peace poured in like a river. From that day forward, "*Christ will do*," became his lifetime motto!

 He was so right! Christ will do! Christ will do for He is the only reconciler of man to God. Christ will do for He alone is the appointed mediator between the sinner and the All-Holy majestic One (1Timothy 2:5). Christ will do for He is the one who poured out His life's blood for sinners (Ephesians 1:7; Ephesians 2:13). Christ will do for He has risen in glorious triumph over the grave (Matthew 28:6). Christ will do for He is the darling of heaven (Revelation 5:8-14). Christ will do for He is heaven's champion (Hebrews 2:10). Christ will do for He is the image of the invisible God (Colossians 1:15), Christ will do for He is the brightness of the Father's glory and the express image of his person (Hebrews 1:3). Christ will do for the Father has had only one crowning purpose, which is to demonstrate His glory and grace in His well beloved Son (Ephesians 2:7). Christ will do for all events are moving towards that day when every knee will bow and every tongue confess that Jesus Christ is the Kurios, the Lord (Philippians 2:9-11).

What a great life motto for us as we learn to look away from ourselves and our supposed sufficiency ---"*Christ will do.*"

What a great folly there is in performing religious works or chasing after religious experiences to get closer to God. If we behave like that, then deep within our hearts we are saying, "Christ will <u>not</u> do!" We can't be any nearer to God than we already are in Christ. What a disaster, then, to chase after new supposed blessings when we are already blessed with all spiritual blessings in heavenly places in Christ (Ephesians 1:3). Yes, Yes, Yes, Christ will do!

And that's the Gospel Truth!

Chapter 17

The Believer's Peace with God

Our peace with God cannot come from our own character because we have none. *"There is none righteous no not one'* (Romans 3:10). What an indictment --- not even one of us is righteous enough to stand before God in our own merit! The truth is this, before we were saved, we were lost with a capital 'L' (Psalm 9:15). We desperately needed a divine intervention. Yet, in spite of the facts, we so easily forget that it was Grace and Mercy which rescued us (Isaiah 51:1; Psalm 40:2), and consequently, almost unconsciously, go about trying to establish our own righteousness (Romans 10:3). We so quickly overlook the fact that, in spite of all God's past dealings with us, we are continually dependent on Him and His power. We stand constantly in need His daily grace and mercy … mercy to keep us from getting what we deserve (judgment) and grace to give us what we don't deserve (continued favour with God).

Concerning grace and mercy there are three things we need to know.

(1) That we continually need both of them
(2) That we do not deserve either of them
(3) That we cannot get them by our own effort

These are three basic, yet easily forgotten, truths!

So how do we continually enjoy our full acquittal before the all-holy God? Is it found in re-doubling our religious efforts and by thinking good things about the Almighty? Or is it by praying harder? Or is it by a little bit of self-sacrifice here and a little bit there? Indeed no! It is by faith alone in Christ alone! No amount of activity, even sincere activity, can persuade God to smile upon us with His favour. Why? Because, our recommendation before God is never found in what we have in ourselves, but in what we don't have. It is our deficiency, not our fullness that has moved God towards us (Exodus 3:7-8). Likewise, just as it is our sickness, not our health, that qualifies us for the doctor, so it is only when we realize how our best efforts are fatally flawed that we can look to Christ alone to be our entire righteousness.

Do we really know that, as believers, we continually need grace and mercy? Do we really know that we don't deserve either of them? And do we know that we still cannot get either of them by our own efforts? Do we know that the crucified Christ is entirely sufficient to mediate between us and the all-holy God of Heaven?

My guilt is great, but greater
The mercy thou dost give
Thyself, a spotless Offering
Hast died that I should live

On Thee my heart is resting
Ah this is rest indeed
What else almighty Saviour
Can a poor sinner need?

In all false religion, the worshipper rests his hope of divine favour upon something within his own character, life or performance. The Pharisee did this when he went into the temple and thanked God that he was not as other men (Luke 18:11). So today, there are those who think that they can maintain right standing with God by doing, feeling, and praying more than they used to. They call themselves Christians, but they are strangers to the gospel. They think that, by their efforts, they can coax or oblige God to grant them favour and furthermore, they feel that God would be grossly unfair to reject people so earnest and devout as they.

These self-righteous religionists place confidence in neither Christ's character nor His finished work. In their madness, they rest in themselves and their efforts, thus rejecting the Christ of God as their only hope. They refuse the one who alone is mighty to save (Isaiah 63:1) and thus they will perish.

And that's the Gospel Truth!

Chapter 18

The New Experience and the Gospel.

We've talked about how self-righteous, religious people prefer their own work and character to that of Christ's. They place confidence in themselves rather than in the doing and dying of Christ alone! They reject that a sinner's resting place is totally outside of himself in the person of Christ (Ephesians 1:6-7). They openly refuse Christ, choosing religious observances, good works, prayers, and devotions, thinking that by such, in combination with upright and decent lives, they have a claim to the mercy of God if indeed they need mercy at all!

But there are also others who are gripped by a different, but equally dangerous deception. These are they who think that by receiving a second blessing, or a series of such, that they find a fuller acceptance from God than the rest of us. Their experiences, they think, bring them to a new level of spirituality and, thus, make them more favoured by the Divine Majesty. In their religious rigor and enthusiasm, they imagine themselves to have supplemented the gospel and secretly think that they are now, because of their experience, more acceptable in heaven than other mere mortals who are relying only on the blood.

Failing to grasp that when Christ is received, all is received (Ephesians 1:3) they now think they have advanced beyond the rest of us. By this kind of philosophy, they both leave and deny the gospel!

An inner experience is never a good substitute for the, outside of us, righteousness of Christ. Consider this; in their "new and enhanced" experiences of supposed new-found spirituality, these "Super Christians" are actually resting on something within them as the supposed means of gaining favour with God. No spiritual experience, however, can furnish the foundation for God's acceptance. Neither regeneration, nor second blessings, nor baptisms, no matter how profound and supposedly life transforming, can be any part of the ground of our approval before the Father. Unless the Lamb had shed His blood, we would be entirely lost and unaccepted in heaven (Hebrews 9:12). However, because of the blood, all blessings such as redemption, peace, forgiveness, justification, and admission into heaven are ours (Ephesians 1:3). This rules out spiritual experiences as being the thing that God requires to gain His acceptance. We are already fully accepted by the Father because of the experiences of the God/Man on our behalf.

We are accepted because of the objective, concrete, saving acts of God, in Christ, in history. The Father has nothing more powerful in store for us than that which He has already done for us in Christ Jesus. For us, Calvary is a historical fact, but for God it is an eternal one. Christ Crucified has been the centre of His heart from before the beginning. The saving acts of God were so far outside of the sinner that they were both planned from eternity and accomplished apart from us two thousand years ago. This is Christianity. It is the only truly historical religion for all other religions teach that salvation is found in some process or experience within the worshiper.

Consequently, in this set up, the worshiper's supreme preoccupation is with himself. What a disaster then to note the countless numbers of Christian songs and sermons that focus us on our experiences and heart condition. They are just another part of the slippery slope that seems determined to remove us from the gospel.

Gospel centred Christianity alone proclaims a salvation which is found in an event outside the believer. We are called, therefore, to occupy ourselves with Christ, the risen and exalted Christ, the crucified Christ who is now alive forevermore (Hebrews 12:2).

By grace alone, the blood of Christ has removed our condemnation, and in the Father's gracious, righteous and loving plan, the blood of Christ has both reconciled us and made us welcome. The blood of Christ has met all claims against us and has brought us to God (Ephesians 2:13).

Acceptance with God is now spelt with five letters----JESUS! We are accepted because of Him alone, not because of our experiences and feelings.

No spiritual experiences can match the experiences the Lord Christ had for us. No experience we can have can heal the breach between sinners and God. The only experience that brings us our acceptance before God is the unique, never to be repeated experience of the Lord Jesus on our behalf.

And that's the Gospel Truth!

Chapter 19

Don't Be Deceived! Part 1

It is impossible for flawed and failed sinners to use worship as a means of gaining the Lord's acceptance. The unsaved cannot worship their way out of condemnation and into the welcome embrace of God (Philippians 3:4-8). Acceptable worship can only come from worshipers who have already become accepted; worshipers who have been declared righteous ...worshipers whose sins have been taken away by the Lamb of God (John 1:29).

Furthermore, for the unregenerate, condemned, religious sinner to occupy himself with religious observances and works in an effort to secure God's favour is the height of arrogant silliness. Instead of his worship and work being the acts of an accepted man, they are the futile attempts of an unaccepted man to gain God's approval. Because of this, his very religious acts are damnable for they make a mockery of the gospel. Indeed, since his prayers are offered to impress God, his prayers become a poisonous and putrid stench emanating from his mouth (Proverbs 28:9). It's not a pretty picture!

God is not impressed by feeble, faltering attempts to verbally flatter Him. Nor is the Lord sympathetic to religious actions, designed to make Him sit up and take notice of the worshipper. On man's part, these actions are nothing less than manifestations of his self-righteousness and, as such, are thoroughly rejected by the Lord. God cannot be bribed; He cannot be coaxed or cajoled by the prayers, works or worship (Matthew 6:5). The Father, however, is already thrilled and well satisfied with the work of the Son on our behalf. He, thus, frowns in severe displeasure and disdain upon those who dismiss His free gift of Christ in favour of their fatally, flawed efforts.

Since repetition is the price of learning, let's say it again, God has already paid the price to bring sinners to Himself and that price is the blood of the Lord Jesus Christ (1 Corinthians 6:20; 1Corinthians 7:23). There is, therefore, nothing more that can now be done to win God's favour and acceptance. This is good news! Christ's payment for our sins is enough! It is satisfactory (Romans 3:22-26)! To base our acceptance before God on our good works, feelings or praying, would be to delude ourselves into thinking that we have right standing with God when there is none. To attempt to find spiritual rest by looking to our own character and religious actions is like a thirsty man trying to quench his thirst with salt and vinegar. Our religious life is a treacherous foundation on which to rest. However the gospel believer can declare,

"Lamb of God we bow before Thee,
Humbly trusting in Thy cross;
That alone be all our glory;
All things else are dung and dross;

Thee we own a perfect Saviour,
Only source of all that's good;
Every grace and every favour
Comes to us through Jesus' blood"

Even if there are many good things about us that can recommend us to others, our good deeds cannot wipe out our record of sin. Also, we should never forget God's verdict that declares what we are like by nature (see Jeremiah 17:9). That one verse alone is enough to make us continually flee to Christ for shelter and salvation. Do not be deceived; the only righteousness that God accepts is that of Christ Jesus and the only way to make that righteousness ours is by faith alone.

 But you say, "I know this, I've heard all this before." To which I humbly reply, "Then hear it again, you will probably forget it within a few moments!" Listen again to the good news. As believers we are already accepted, not because of our efforts, but because of Christ's doing and dying. He is our Saviour, our redemption, protector and security. His arms are underneath us and round about us (Deuteronomy 33:27). He keeps us safe in Him. He died, was buried, has risen again, and ever-lives to make intercession for us. What a wonderful Saviour!

 Be careful, therefore, to avoid any self-made peace that comes from thinking good things about yourself and your efforts. Yes, by all means, live for His glory, but be careful not to be deceived into thinking that your diligent efforts present the Lord with the secure basis for His acceptance. That acceptance is found in Christ alone.

And that's the Gospel Truth!

Chapter 20

Don't Be Deceived! Part 2

Religious people often deceive themselves by saying, *"I don't have many sins and besides that my sins are not too terribly serious, therefore, God will accept me."* Others say, *"I know I've sinned, but I have compensated for my sins by my good deeds, therefore, at the end of the day I should be fine."* Others say, *"I have a very deep sense of sin, therefore, I am guaranteed of acceptance before God."* Another says, *"I have repented of my sin; I can rest on that."* Another says, *"I pray a lot, work a lot, give a lot, and, therefore, I expect God to welcome me."*

All these things, however, are treacherous man-centered foundations of sinking sand. Nowhere has God called us to rely on anything we do or have done to gain His acceptance. Christ Jesus alone is our salvation. He has already been delivered for our offences and has been raised for our justification (Romans 4:25). There is, therefore, nothing that we can contribute to the powerful, saving acts of God in Christ alone.

Christ has finished His work and is now in heaven. As He reigns in glory, He is our righteousness, our right standing before the Father, and our storehouse of inexhaustible blessings. It is Christ alone, with nothing added, who is our righteousness before the Father. Our peace and confidence are built upon Him alone, and not on anything that we do or have done. Yes I know, we so easily drift back to looking for something to add to Christ and His work for us. However, genuine faith rests upon the saving acts of God in Christ alone!

We need to understand that, true peace and confidence before God cannot come from our character or performance. Indeed to think that we can perform well enough to impress God, is to have a very high, self-righteous view of ourselves, and an equally low opinion of God's holy and just requirements.

"Yes," but you say, *"everything I do is empowered by God's Spirit --- surely I can rest on the Spirit's work within me as the ground of confidence before*

God?" In one aspect, this seems like a good idea, but like so many seemingly good ideas, it is fatally flawed. For example, I suppose that, at the time, Abraham thought that Ishmael was a good idea, but of course he couldn't see the future consequence of his actions. Likewise, when we look to the work of the Spirit as the ground of our justification, we are setting a disastrous course, for we are looking to something within us as the foundation of our peace! Is the Holy Spirit's work within us finished? Absolutely not! His work within us is ongoing and is, therefore, not completed. How foolish then to rest upon an incomplete work as our ground of acceptance before the Father.

Our acceptance, however, is entirely outside of us, in Christ alone and His finished completed accomplishments. Because of this, saving faith is never turned in on ourselves, rather it is focused outside of us on the Lord Jesus Christ (Galatians 5:5). Faith accepts that acceptance is ours in Christ alone! Nowhere in Scripture are we told to look to the inward work of the Spirit as the foundation and ground of our peace before God! We receive the gift of the Spirit (Ephesians 2:8), not to give us the ground of peace and acceptance, but because Christ, our substitute, has died, resurrected and been accepted in our place!

Often, when we become preoccupied with what God is doing in us, we quickly lose sight of what he has already done for us in the person and work of the Lord Jesus. This is a sure and certain way to depart from the gospel!

And that's the Gospel Truth!

Chapter 21

Adding to the Sufficiency of the Gospel

When, as believers, we forget the gospel, we usually resort to futile and useless attempts to supplement the grace of God. We, almost unconsciously, do little extra things to try to secure the Lord's favour. But, this kind of behaviour places us in direct opposition to the cross of Christ. It is just another way of snubbing the Lord. We, in actuality, by our efforts to show how worthy we are, are saying that the grace found in Christ's doing and dying is insufficient to recommend us to the Father.

In the Bible, God has declared himself to be gracious (Nehemiah 9:31) and has embodied this grace in the person and work of the Son (Titus 2:11). He has told us that gospel grace is for the ungodly, the unholy and the unfit, (Romans 5:6, 8, 10). The more, then, that we know (A) the grace of Christ Jesus and (B) our inability to produce anything that will recommend us to God, the more we will thrive on the gospel and cease trying to impress God and others.

Here's some good news, believers are already complete in Christ (Colossians 2:10). We may at times disappoint and devastate ourselves with personal failures and hardness of heart, but the greatness of our sin, although it may humble us, cannot remove us from the completeness we have in the Lord Jesus. In fact, failure can actually help us by breaking us of our pride. A broken believer quickly learns to be wary of any supposed righteousness within him masquerading as the ground of his acceptance before the Lord. God is still the God of Romans 8:28!

May the Lord break us, and teach us the sufficiency of the gospel. May we continually grasp that our acceptance with the Father neither comes from our own efforts nor from thinking inflated things about ourselves. Let's face it, everything we do is flawed. Even our best works are riffled with impure motives (Isaiah 64:6). Looking to our accomplishments, therefore, can never bring peace with God. True peace of conscience, however, comes from the person and work of Christ for us. As we continually apprehend Him as our substitutionary representative, we are set free from the endless process of trying to secure God's favour by our puny, little, useless efforts.

In Christ alone, we meet God and His sufficiency. In the gospel, we discover that He has done something about our sin and predicament. In the gospel, we see that God is for us … this is astonishing! If God didn't care about our condition, we would have good reason to panic and despair. I'm sure you'll agree, it would be a shattering and devastating truth to discover that God was against us! It would be a frightful thing to encounter God as an enemy and not a friend! But, we no longer have to live in dread of the Almighty. Nor do we have to think that, when we are not looking over our shoulder, He is going to reach out of heaven and strike us down. As believers, we no longer have to try to impress Him by our furious religious activity. The gospel delivers us from such redundant thought.

The Bible says that God is love, not hate! The good news of His love, was fully revealed in the cross where the Lord Jesus took upon Himself the sins of His people (Matthew 1:27). As believers, to think that we can now impress the Lord with our best efforts and thus somehow move Him to favour us is to fail to grasp the gospel. It is very opposite of what the Bible teaches. We need to continually turn our eyes back to Calvary and from there to the Throne of Grace. As we do, we will notice that there are no threats being issued against us from the Lamb of God.

And that's the Gospel Truth!

Chapter 22

Gospel Grace

As we learn to be 'Gospel Driven' and not 'Law Directed', we have the privilege to absorb ourselves in the powerful knowledge that God Himself came to this earth as our personal representative. As such, He not only substituted for us in His death, but also in His life. When He was declared 'beloved', we were declared beloved. When He was punished, we were punished; when he rose from the dead we rose from the dead.

As He is accepted so are we accepted; as He is accepted and loved, so we are accepted and loved. We are now in Him and are now blessed with all spiritual blessings in the heavenly places (Ephesians 1:3).

When Jesus hung on the cross God's disfavour towards us rested on Him and now, because of Calvary, God's favour rests on us. Knowing the immensity then of the grace we have received, how is it that we can be un-gracious and mean to those whom we feel have sinned against us? How strange is that? The gospel, however, when embraced, releases us to be kind, tender hearted and forgiving (Ephesians 4:32).

As we steep ourselves in the gospel and its applications, we come to appreciate more and more of the grace that has been given to us in Christ and because of this we become more gracious. By the gospel, we are enabled not only to abandon our own righteousness, but also to see that, because of grace alone, we are now reckoned as being perfectly righteous with neither perverseness nor iniquity reckoned to us (Numbers 23:21). May we be helped to do the same for those who have sinned against us and who are now seeking our mercy?

We are saved by the immense grace of the eternal God which has appeared in the person of Jesus Christ (Titus 2:11; John 1:14). Our redeemer is full of grace and truth" and "of His fullness we have all received and grace for grace" (John 1:16). Literally we have received grace "piled upon" grace. Just as there are continual arrivals of waves on the seashore, so we are continually receiving wave upon wave of God's inexhaustible grace in Christ

Jesus. Jesus is the grace of God in human form. His grace is Glorious (Ephesians 1:6). Abundant (Acts 4:33); Rich (Ephesians 1:7). Manifold (many-sided). (1 Peter 4:10) and Sufficient (there is never a shortage) (2 Corinthians 12:9).

Surely then, in the light of these gospel truths we can learn to be gracious one to another? You see it's one thing to know the words of the song of grace, but quite another to know the melody.

The following is a great illustration of the application of gospel grace.
In the 1800s, London had two exceedingly famous preachers, Charles Spurgeon and Joseph Parker. On one occasion, Parker commented about the poor condition of children admitted to Spurgeon's orphanage. Word of this came to Spurgeon, but by the time it arrived, it was reported to Spurgeon that Parker had criticized the orphanage itself. Spurgeon blasted Parker from his pulpit and the attack was printed in the newspaper and became the talk of the town. Londoners flocked to Parker's church the next Sunday to hear his rebuttal.

Here's what Parker said,

"I understand Mr Spurgeon is not in his pulpit today, and this is the Sunday they use to take an offering for the orphanage," Parker said. "I suggest we take a love offering for the orphanage."
The crowd was delighted; ushers had to empty the collection plates three times. Later that week, there was a knock at Parker's study. It was Spurgeon.

"You know, Parker, you have practiced grace on me," he said. "You have given me not what I deserved; you have given me what I needed."

May we all have the grace to live as though the gospel is real and that grace has indeed arrived in the person of Jesus the Christ.

And that's the Gospel Truth!

Chapter 23

The Man Who Prayed in Reverse

When Simon Peter saw his wretchedness, he fell down at Jesus' knees, saying, "Depart from me I am a sinful man O Lord" (Luke 5:8).

It was only when the big fisherman, Simon Peter, was confronted with the awesome power and majesty of Christ that he began to see the extent of his wicked sinfulness. But look at his strange response to this awful discovery---he asked the Lord to depart from him. He's the man who prayed in reverse. He prayed backwards!

What a strange gospel it would be if our sin caused the Lord to depart. It was our sin which brought Him here in the first place. Do we now think that our sin will drive Him away? Have we gone so far from the gospel that we imagine there is a throne of grace from which we must run and hide? Or do we imagine that we must clean and reform our ways before we are fit to approach the Master? Does our sin, like Peter's, make us want to avoid the Lord Christ? Unfortunately, this is often the case.

Instead of praying, "Depart from me," Peter should have prayed, "Lord come to me and let me come to you for I am a sinful man. I need you Lord. I'm a sinner, please forgive me, heal my conscience, remove my guilt and strengthen me."

By learning to embrace the grace and mercy which is in Christ, the gospel believer becomes a prayer warrior. The gospel believer knows that his sin is so awful that there is nothing but the blood of Christ which can open the way to heaven. The gospel believer knows something of the power and authority of the blood. He knows that there is nothing but the blood which can bring Him to the throne of God (Ephesians 2:13; Hebrews 10:19). The gospel believer can, therefore, confidently agree that the best place for him is with the Saviour of Sinners and not away from Him!

But in spite of knowing these wonderful gospel truths, our sin, like that of Adam's, tends to make us want to hide. As Shakespeare said, "Conscience does make cowards of us all." Sometimes we are too afraid to go to the throne of grace. We know we deserve, not favour, but frowns and we wonder how we can as sinful people go to God with boldness?

So how we do it? How do we go there? Here's the answer. As justified believers, we walk by faith. Faith sees that we have a great High Priest sitting, not on a throne of wrath and fury, but on a throne of grace. Faith then sees that this priest is our Saviour of sinners who embraces us with His welcome. Faith sees that, in our nature and as our personal representative, the Royal High Priest lived a holy and sinless life on our behalf. Faith sees that He was also crucified and killed, yet faith also sees that He rose again, ascended and sat down on His throne in Heaven. Faith holds out it's hand and receives welcoming grace, mercy and cleansing. Faith brings us boldly to the throne of grace and not away from it.

Faith also sees that we are, not only invited to the throne of grace, but are actually commanded to come to it. Faith gives us confidence to go there for faith sees that Christ Himself is our confidence. In Him we find, not man's mercy, but God's.

And that's the Gospel Truth!

Chapter 24

Not Satisfied?

If salvation required that our faith, love and repentance had to have a sufficiently high level before the Lord accepted us, none of us would ever have been saved. Take, for example, the matter of faith. Does God require us to have a set level of feeling in our faith before He saves us? Of course not!   He neither asks us to feel lost nor saved, for if He did, none of us would know whether or not we ever felt lost or saved enough. He does, however, want us to know that outside of Jesus, we are lost (Romans 5:12) ---we don't have to feel this! He wants us to know this and believe this, for this is what His Word teaches. His word is enough to persuade us of the truth apart from feelings (Proverbs 30:5).

The gospel needs no authentication from our emotions. The Scriptures are true whether or not we feel them to be true (Psalm 33:4). Faith knows this and latches on to the truth! Faith, not feelings, knows that, in Christ, there is everything we need for our salvation (2 Corinthians 9:8; 2 Corinthians 3:5: 2 Corinthians 12:9)."

Furthermore, on this question of loving God, I've heard Christians say, "I don't think I love God enough." Well, what did they expect? Do you know of anyone who has a perfect love for the Father other than the Lord Jesus? Now here's some good gospel truth; since we have been reckoned as having Christ's perfect righteousness then, in Him, we have already loved the Father perfectly. This is wonderful! Does this not release you to love the Father more? Or are you now walking contrary to gospel by demanding a perfect love from yourself? The bigger issue, however, is not your love for Him, but rather, Christ's love for the Father on your behalf.

As for this matter of repentance, some folks feel that they haven't repented enough. Shock! Horror! None of us has! And do you know what? If we were satisfied with our repentance, no one could put up with us for we would be filled with all manner of pride and self-righteousness. Repentance is a vital truth, but do you think that God will take note of your repentance and on the basis of such forgive your sins? Is your repentance greater than the blood? Do you think that your repentance can atone for your sins and purchase God's favour? If all that is needed to secure salvation is repentance, then Christ could have stayed in Heaven and not bothered with the cross.

So tell me this, on what basis would you rather approach the thrice-holy God, with your repentance or with the Lamb's blood? Do you think your repentance now gives you that which only Christ can provide? Are you still trying to find the ground of peace in the perfections of your repentance? If so, you are yet in the grip of self-righteousness!

As a young, but learned clergyman, James Hervey, the 18th century English preacher asked an old ploughman what he though was the hardest thing in religion. The old man replied that Hervey was a learned man and that he would like to know what he thought on that subject. "Well," said Hervey, "I think it is to deny sinful self. "I disagree," said the old Christian, "I think there is a harder thing than that and that is to deny righteous self-----to deny ourselves a proud dependence on our own works and struggles and efforts and prayers for justification before God." Hervey afterwards said that, at the time, he thought the ploughman an old fool; but, said he, "I have since learned who was the fool---not the pious ploughman, but the proud James Hervey" (Galatians 2:21).

Christ alone is our resting place. To be satisfied with Him is enough, for He is enough!

And that's the Gospel Truth!

Chapter 25

True and Unimagined Peace

True and unimagined peace comes only as we understand God's character. If we erroneously envision God to be permanently angry and frowning, we will neither know the Lord nor His perfect peace. If we falsely picture that we have to perform continually to gain His favour and approval, life will be an uninterrupted, emotional upheaval. If we mistakenly imagine that God, having purchased us by His blood (Acts 20:28), will someday wither in His faithfulness and desert us, we will be tossed to and fro by every circumstance and trial. To enjoy true peace reigning in our hearts, however, we need to be fastened firmly to the rock of the objective gospel of the doing and dying of Christ.

Our understanding of the gospel is vital for many reasons, including the following one. Being holy, the Holy Spirit will neither bless the worship of a false God nor the false worship of the true God. But who is the living and true God? The living and true God is the, "the God of all grace"(1 Peter 5:10), He is the God of the gospel (Romans 1:1) and it is the love of this one true God that the Spirit sheds abroad in our hearts (Romans 5:5).

Nor does the Holy Spirit produce false feelings in us so that we can go around thinking wonderful things about ourselves ... things which might establish a false confidence before the Lord. He continues to destroy every vestige of self-righteousness as He causes us see that we are saved from beginning to end by grace alone through faith alone in Christ alone.

The grace of God destroys all our supposed works and self-worthiness, yet it comes to us without cost to us or cause in us. It is absolutely free, or it is not at all (Romans 4:4, 16; Ephesians 2:8-9; 2 Timothy 1:9).

The object of the Spirit's work is to bring us to an understanding of the gracious and righteous character of God as demonstrated by the doing and dying of Christ. As we encounter God in Christ, we learn to rest in Him. As we grow in grace, the Holy Spirit continues to show us our innate lostness and at the same time the security we have in Christ's finished work for us. He does not enable us to feel or believe, in order that we can have false comfort by our feelings or even our faith. He does not cause us to place false hope in our supposed progress in the Christian faith, but rather works in us turning our eyes away from His own work and fixing them on the love of God in Christ Jesus for us.

May the power of grace by the Spirit continually turn our eyes to see the cross and the Crucified One. Let us never forget who this crucified One is. He is God Himself; incarnate love hanging upon a cross. He is the God who created us, the master architect of the universe, suffering and dying for the ungodly. Can you question His commitment to you? Can you ask anything further to bring you to the place of wholehearted trust and confidence? It is no wonder that we read, "*Hereby perceive we the love of God, that he laid down his life for us.*" (1 John 3:16) "*Herein is love, not that we love God, but that he loved us, and sent his Son to be the propitiation of our sins.*" (1 John 4:10). As the Puritan, Tomas Watson observed,

"The emperor Trajan tore off a piece of his robe to bind up one of his soldier's wounds. But Christ tore off His own flesh for us! "He gave Himself for us to redeem us" (Titus 2:14).

Christ gave Himself for us …. what more could He give?

"Lamb of God, we fall before Thee,
Humbly trusting in Thy cross.
That alone be all our glory;
All things else are only dross.

Thee we own a perfect Saviour,
Only source of all that's good.
Every grace and every favour
Comes to us through Jesus' blood.

And that's the Gospel Truth!

Chapter 26

The Greatest Trading Post in the World

In the cross of Christ, we find the greatest trading post in the world. There, our filthy robes of self-righteousness were traded for Christ's robe of perfect righteousness (Isaiah 61:10). Our guilt was traded for grace and mercy, and our condemnation was traded for our justification. This is not make-believe or some kind of legal fiction. This is reality (Hebrews 9:22; 1 Peter 2:24).

As believers, all of Christ's righteousness is credited to us. Did you catch that? ALL of Christ's righteousness is reckoned to us. In the gospel, we are not given a righteousness that looks like Christ's or one that is similar to Christ's, we are given Christ's very own righteousness. All of His perfection, in all its completeness, is now reckoned as being ours. This is no empty theory; this is gospel. Live in it and enjoy it. At the cross, Christ Jesus took legal liability for us and gave us the gift of His righteousness. This is such good and powerful news that, if this gospel were continually preached and believed in our churches, then believers would be transformed and delivered from lives that so often entangle and entrap them.

There are many whom I've met who, in their flesh, are striving after their own brand of holiness. They fail to realize that the all-holy God requires perfection. These folk, neither understand true holiness nor the true nature of sin. They, therefore, go about trying to meet what they suppose to be God's standard. To them Christianity is about keeping the rules and trying to impress God and man. Failing to grasp the gospel fact that Christ has already reached God's standard on our behalf, these folks are doomed to live lives of misery and failure. The only way they can live a so called perfect life is to either lower the standard of perfection or to excuse sin as not being sin at all! As a result, they lie to themselves about having reached a higher state than the rest of us. Some of them are so deceived that they believe they can actually live throughout the day without sin. They know nothing of the 'Gospel Trading Post'.

As believers, we must have a good understanding of the Trading Post of the cross. There we encounter the righteousness of God in Christ.

Everything that God requires of us is met in Christ; it is supplied in Christ and is fulfilled in Christ. God demands perfection, and the believer has that in Christ. God demands full and total obedience, and we have that in Christ.

Horatius Bonar, in his book, "The Everlasting Righteousness" comments on Ezekiel 16 saying, "Although the prophet was speaking of Jerusalem we can apply his words to believers. The word of the Lord to us through Ezekiel is choice. The Lord says,

1. "I said to you, Live" (Ezekiel 16: verse 6).
2. "I spread my skirt over thee" (verse 8).
3. "I entered into a covenant with you, and you became mine"
(verse 8).
4. "I washed you" (verse 9).
5. "I anointed you" (verse 9).
6. "I clothed you" (verse 10).
7. "I shod you" (verse 10).
8. "I girded you" (verse 10).
9. "I covered you with silk" (verse 10).
10. "I decked you with ornaments, bracelets, chains, jewels, a
beautiful crown" (verse 12).
11. "You were exceeding beautiful" (verse 13).

12. "Your renown went forth for your beauty" (verse 14).
This is a snapshot of the 'Trading Post' and the perfection with which we, as believers, are now clothed. The Lord Himself is our righteousness and He says to us, "Thou art all fair, my love; there is no spot in thee" (Song of Songs 4:7). As we believe this, we enter into rest.

And that's the Gospel Truth!

Chapter 27

The Sufficiency of the Saviour

As the gospel is applied, we discover to our utter delight that, "He that believes is not condemned" (John 3:18). This is actually looking at the negative side of things for it tells us what we are not rather than what we are! However, even if this were the entirety of gospel benefits, it would be thrilling, for as P.T. Forsyth says,

"As a race, we're not even stray sheep, or wandering prodigals, we are rebels taken with weapons in our hands." (Forsyth, Peter Taylor; Positive Preaching and Modern Mind; p 56).

To know that all possibility of condemnation has been lifted is both stunning and liberating. Have you told yourself this powerful gospel truth lately? Have you had a good talk with yourself about how you are no longer under condemnation? "He that believes is not condemned," says the Word of the Lord. Is this verse talking about you? Are you a believer? Are you relying on Christ alone? If so, you are not condemned. You will never be damned

(Romans 8:1). Christ Jesus is the sufficient Saviour. His person, work and offices guarantee that there is no condemnation for you. Christ's sufficiency is not in question. The question is, however, are you relying on Him and His sufficiency alone? Is He your substitute in life and death? If He is, let's say it again, you will never be damned!

But there's more! Because of His sufficiency, the benefits of the gospel are even bigger. Not only will believers not be damned, but because of the sufficiency of the Saviour, believers are also, "made the righteousness of God in Him" (2 Corinthians 5:21). Furthermore, "Christ is the end (or fulfilling) of the law for righteousness to every one that believes" (Romans 10:4). That means our acceptance before God does not come through our own efforts at Law keeping.

We are now the righteousness of God in Christ. We have this on good authority ... an authority that cannot lie ... God's Word.
And not only so, but having been declared righteous, we have also been embraced and welcomed by heaven. We are now accepted in the beloved (Ephesians 1:6).

But why and how is this possible? It is for this simple yet profound reason; when Christ lived and died, He demonstrated His perfect obedience and unswerving, unshakeable love for the Father. Being now found in Him we are reckoned as having the same unerring love and obedience. It is credited to us by free grace alone!

The Scripture doesn't say we must have a strong faith or even a great faith to receive these truths. Faith, it must be remembered, is not a work, nor is it something we earn or produce ourselves. On the contrary, it is when we end our works and receive Christ in place of them that we are actually walking by faith. However, we do not depend on our faith to save us. Christ alone is the Saviour. Christ alone saves sinners.

Are you worried that your faith is not strong enough? Again we must neither look at ourselves nor the weakness or strength of our faith; we must look, rather, to the cross of Calvary and the sufficiency of the One who died on our behalf! It was Christ Jesus the Lord who suffered for sin, the just for the unjust that He might bring us to God (1 Peter 3:18). Has He brought you to God? He has? Then rest on that. Jesus is the living way Who calls us to have no faith in ourselves, but rather confidence in Him. In Him, we have obtained right of access to Heaven for in Him we are the righteousness of God. His perfection is sufficient to cover righteously, not only that which is imperfect in our characters and lives, but also that which is imperfect in our faith. As the old Hymn writer once said,

"Had I an angel's righteousness
I'd lay aside that beauteous dress,
And wrap me up in Christ."

And that's the Gospel Truth!

Chapter 28

Gospel Acquittal

Because of the gospel, we have been, not merely pardoned for sins, but totally acquitted and declared not guilty. Do you see the difference?

I read once of how a man who had been in prison for a crime was brought before the Judge. The prisoner had had a profound change of life. He had served much time and was now a reformed man. The Judge heard the facts and because of the prisoner's change of character, issued him a pardon. It was a lovely story, but it's quite unlike the gospel. You see, there is nothing in us that deserves any kind of mercy. We are all guilty before the thrice-holy, supreme majesty! The apostle Paul spoke for us all when he said, "I know that in me, that is in my flesh, dwells no good thing" (Romans 7:18). None of us deserve any favour or mercy from God! We all should be condemned.

Our salvation, however, was bought and paid for by Christ, but He purchased much more than our pardon. The pardoned man in our story was still a guilty man, but the acquitted man is not guilty of anything! Christ alone bought and secured our acquittal. The declaration from heaven upon us is, therefore, "Not guilty ... case dismissed."

The acquittal or 'not guilty' verdict is ours because the Father has given us the same verdict He gave to His Son (Romans 2:13). Because Christ was our substitute in His life and death, the Father's verdict on Christ is automatically ours. Christ lived and died as our willing substitute. Because of this, when He was born sinlessly, we were born sinlessly. When He lived sinlessly, we lived sinlessly, and when He poured out His blood for our sins, He died as though He were us. "The Lord has laid on Him the iniquity of us all" (Isaiah 53:6). This is exceptionally good news.

"Oh," you say, "how I wish I could feel that." I understand you and can sympathise, but the facts are these, you don't have to feel, "not guilty" to be not guilty. When someone is acquitted in court, they receive their verdict, not by feelings, but, rather, by the word of the Judge. In heaven's court, God the Judge has declared us not guilty.

The Lord said it; that settles it; I believe it; that settles me!

As we learn to take God at His word about our acquittal, the feelings of guilt flee. We rest in the word of the God who cannot lie (Titus 1:2). We may be the feeblest believer who has ever walked the face of the earth, but if Christ is our Saviour, we now enjoy the freedom of the, not guilty verdict. He has put our sins behind His back (Isaiah 38:17). Indeed, "As far as the East is from the West so far has He removed our transgressions from us" (Psalms 103:12).

Acquittal is a gospel mercy which we take by sheer faith. No one has ever seen God blotting out their sin, and no one has ever heard the declaration of the "not guilty" verdict, but we believe it has been done because the Lord Christ has said, "It is Finished" (John 19:30).
The knowledge that our sins are no longer charged against us is wonderful, but knowing that they are forgotten is even better. Hebrews 10:17 says, "And their sins and iniquities will I remember no more." If they are forgotten by God, what are we doing digging them up and remembering them?

The wisdom of this world says, "Blessed is the man who is rich and powerful." But the wisdom of the Lord says, "Blessed is the man whose transgression is forgiven and whose sin is covered; blessed is the man to whom the lord imputes not iniquity and in whose spirit is no guile" (Psalms 32:1-2).

And that's the Gospel Truth!

Chapter 29

Gospel Righteousness

The gospel truth of Justification means that every charge against the believer has been dropped. As the scripture declares, "Who shall lay anything to the charge of God's elect? It is God that justifies" (Romans 8:33). There are no accusations that can stand against the Lord's sheep because they have been declared not guilty in the courtroom of God. But there's more!

Justification goes far beyond being cleared of guilt. When we are justified, we are not only acquitted, but also declared righteous. This is a necessary truth for not only does the Law forbid sin, it also demands righteousness. But where do we find a righteousness that satisfies the Father? Some people reason that regeneration is the solution for this. However, vital as regeneration is, it cannot provide perfect righteousness. The flesh still lusts against the spirit (Galatians 5:17).

In addition, the "not guilty" declaration, although essential, does not, and cannot, clothe us with righteousness. It declares us innocent, but there is a significant difference between being innocent and being righteous! The truth is this, the man who is declared not guilty is still unworthy in himself. Everything he does is flawed, imperfect and defiled by sin.

But here's the good news, gospel justification not only declares us not guilty, but also declares us righteous. We are now accepted before God having, not only been washed in the blood of Christ, but also by having Christ's righteousness reckoned as being ours. Martyn Lloyd Jones says,

"In justifying us, God tells us that He has taken our sins and our guilt and has "imputed" them to, "put them to the account of," the Lord Jesus Christ and punished them in Him. He announces also that, having done that, He now puts to our account, or "imputes" to us, the perfect righteousness of His own dear Son. The Lord Jesus Christ obeyed the law perfectly; He never broke it in any respect; He gave a full and a perfect satisfaction to all its demands. That full obedience constitutes His righteousness. What God does is to put to our account, to put upon us, the righteousness of Jesus Christ. In declaring us to be justified, God proclaims that He now looks on us, not as we are, but as clothed with the righteousness of the Lord Jesus Christ."

Because of Justification, God looks at us and says that (1) we are not guilty, and (2) we are righteous in Christ. Our past has been legally and justly expunged, and we have been given a totally new identity. It's like being in a witness protection program that is 100% secure!
"Christ is made unto us righteousness." 1 Corinthians 1:30. This is the blessing of grace that belongs to every believer. The Fathers looks at us and see us as righteous in Christ. If a man, however, refuses to submit to this righteousness, he, in his folly, is declaring Christ's righteousness to be superfluous and un-necessary. Furthermore, he is saying that man's righteousness (his in particular) is sufficient for acceptance before God. Such a person is not in the gospel; he will perish.

Jesus, Thy blood and righteousness
My beauty are, my glorious dress;
'Midst flaming worlds, in these arrayed
With joy shall I lift up my head.
Bold shall I stand in that great day,
For who aught to my charge shall lay?

Fully absolved through these I am,
From sin and fear, from guilt and shame.

Some years ago an Irish Farmer stood up to testify at a gospel meeting. He said, "Brothers and Sisters look at me. I'm not a pretty sight. In fact, I'm just a big, old, ugly Irish farmer, but in God's sight I'm altogether lovely for I'm all dressed up in the righteousness of Christ."

This man understood something of the benefits of the gospel.

And that's the Gospel Truth!

Chapter 30

Gospel Adoption

It's good to have all charges against us dropped and even better to be declared righteous, but it's best to have been adopted as children of God. And that's exactly what has happened to us as a result of the gospel. We are now children of God by faith in Christ Jesus (Galatians 3:26). As we look at gospel adoption, we realize that grace has outdone sin, for it has lifted us much, much higher than the place from which we fell.

'Adoption' is a legal term derived from Roman law. There were often two stages to this ancient legal process. In the first stage, a Roman nobleman would identify a child he wanted to adopt and would clothe him with robes appropriate for his new status. The second step came later; it was the public acknowledgment of the adoption whereby the adopted person entered into their full and active rights as a member of the nobility. Just as there was a season during which the privileges of adoption were not fully seen, it is not yet fully seen what we are in Christ. However, there is coming a day when all will be revealed. "Beloved, now are we the sons of God, and it doth not yet appear what we shall be: but we know that, when he shall appear, we shall be like him; for we shall see him as he is (1 John 3:2).

We have been adopted by the Father! Indeed, *"Behold what manner of love the Father has given unto us that we should be called Sons of God"* (1 John 3:1). But why did He do this? Why did He adopt us? The answer is simple and yet at the same time profound. He adopted us simply because He wanted to adopt us, He exercised His free will in the matter. We know this because the Bible says, "Having predestined us unto the adoption of children by Jesus Christ to himself, according to the good pleasure of his will, (Ephesians 1:5).

The privilege of adoption makes us sons of God. Every morning when you look in the mirror you encounter royalty. Oh yes I know that you also encounter a wretch, however, "You are no more a servant but a son and an heir of God through Christ (Galatians 4:7). This is remarkable, for it means that, as His child, the Father loves us just the same way He loves Christ! It's not, therefore, a presumption for you to say (and to keep saying), "The Father loves me." The fact is, and I don't want to sound irreverent, He's crazy about you! It's hard for us to believe, isn't it?

Too often we don't feel loved because we feel unlovable. We have, as some call it, 'an orphaned heart'! But the more we know the gospel, the more we will realize that we don't have to feel loved. We need to stop trying to feel His love and begin to believe His love. We are His blood bought children, we are in Christ, and we have been loved since before time! Being adopted means that, in and through Christ, we have been given the royal rights of sons of God; the Father loves us as he loves his only-begotten Son. We are now children of God, "And if children, then heirs; heirs of God, and joint-heirs with Christ; if so be that we suffer with him, that we may be also glorified together" (Romans 8:17).

If we are in Christ, we will have all things with Him. If we are His, we shall share the crown with Him. If we are in Christ, we as adopted children will receive the inheritance of the saints in light (Colossians 1:12).

This is remarkable; we who were once heirs of hell have now been adopted and made Heirs of Heaven.

And that's the Gospel Truth!

Chapter 31

Eternal Life

Because of the gospel, we are given life, not for a day or a month or even a year, but given eternal life! That's the way Jesus told it. He said, "My sheep hear my voice ... and I give unto them eternal life" (John 10:27-28).

What a stunning promise! What a splendid gift! Notice how He says "I give." Clearly, if He gives eternal life, that means we didn't have it in the first place. Furthermore, since it's a gift, it stands to reason that we have neither earned nor deserved it.

It has been pointed out by others that the term eternal life also includes an idea of a certain quality of life. If truth be told, Jesus didn't merely promise us eternal existence, He promised something far better ... eternal life.
Part of this life is the absence of condemnation (Romans 8:1). Christ Jesus came into the world on purpose; He came to be condemned in our place. He came so that we would be acquitted, declared

righteous and adopted. He came to give us the gift of Himself ... eternal life (1 John 5:11).

As Christians, living under the gospel transforms and helps us to enjoy the purchase made, by Christ, on our behalf. However, if we live under a religious system devoid of the gospel, a system that urges us to try harder and harder, it only serves to manufacture guilt and death. The truth is, right standing with God, and His gift of eternal life, have nothing whatsoever to do with how we behave.

Someone says, "That's dangerous doctrine brother! People will abuse those things if you preach them." True, some people probably will. But are you saying that because people might misuse these glorious truths that we should not preach them? Listen to me, some years ago my cousin, in Canada, was killed when a snow-laden branch of a tree fell on her. Does this mean that, because they can be dangerous, all trees and forests should be cut down? Also, when I was a child, a young boy from our village, in Ireland, drowned while swimming in the sea! Does that mean we should drain the ocean? Sometimes trees and oceans do terrible things. So it is with people! I'm advocating, however, that in spite of the dangers of potential abuse, that we believers live in and proclaim the gospel and enjoy the wonderful freedom afforded to us by its gospel mercies.

It is only through the gospel that we can enjoy eternal life here and now and out into eternity. Christ Jesus, our gospel, is the giver of eternal life (John 17:2) and we have the privilege of enjoying both Him and His free gift.

There was an old black preacher in Richmond, Virginia, John Jasper, during the American Civil War who preached to very large audiences. People came from everywhere to hear him.

Someone asked him; "When, you get to heaven and they stop you at the door, and ask, what right have you got to be here in this celestial city, in the abode of God, in the majestic heavens, what are you going to say?"

John Jasper replied, "I am going to say; "I ain't got no right to be here at all. I am not here on my rights; I am here on the righteousness of Jesus

Christ my Lord and Saviour. I am here on the mercy of another who gave me eternal life."

What a wonderful reply. Our hope of Heaven is in the Lord's doing, dying and rising again on our behalf. We live, not because of our merit, but because of His mercy.

And that's the Gospel Truth!

Chapter 32

Rich in Mercy

When we think of God, does the truth that He is wonderfully merciful immediately spring to mind? Probably not!
More than likely, when we think of Him, we conjure up a picture of someone who is harsh, critical and judgmental......someone not to run to, but to run from. However, this kind of faulty thinking about the character of the Almighty can have dire consequences. In fact, unless we get our thoughts about God straight, our walk with Him will be crooked.

The scripture declares boldly, in Ephesians 2:4, that God is rich in mercy. Did you know that the Greek word translated 'rich', is the same word from which we get our English word 'plush'. Just think of it, ... our God is plush in mercy. That means, He's not stingy when it comes to mercy. It means that He doesn't dispense mercy with eye drops. No!!! On the contrary, He is rich, plush, extravagant, and liberal when it comes to giving out mercy.

In all my years as a believer, I have not yet encountered a single person who didn't need mercy. Believers and unbelievers alike continually need daily mercy. Every day, as Christians, we sin and fail God. I think you'll agree that we followers of Christ don't pray, love God or love each other the way we should do. We have a continual need of mercy! But God is plush with mercy. He is wealthy in and generous with that mercy. So whatever your situation today, bring it to the One who abounds in mercy.

We may feel like complete failures in our Christian lives ... but God is rich in mercy. Because He is rich in mercy, the God/Man came to earth and was slaughtered at the cross for our entire sinful falling and failing. Because He is rich in mercy, He was set forth and publicly displayed as a propitiation (a wrath offering) for us. Because He is rich in mercy, He has become the very Mercy Seat for the fallen believer. So let's not run from Him ... instead, run to Him! He is rich in mercy!

Regardless of how much we have failed Him, we can come to Him today, right now, for mercy. Perhaps you are saying to yourself, "I don't deserve mercy." Well, truer words were never spoken! Think of it, if any of us deserved it, it wouldn't be mercy.

His mercy is great. His grace is free. He is rich in mercy. May we never, ever let shame trick us into staying away from Him. Staying away will only lead to straying away.

Spurgeon tells of how the gospel preacher, Rowland Hill, was given a large sum of money to dispense to a certain minister who was extremely poor. In his wisdom, Mr Hill realised that if he were to give him the entire sum of money all at once, the poor minister would be overwhelmed. So he decided to send the money in instalments every few days and with each instalment he wrote a note to the minister which simply said, "There's more to follow."

This is so like the blessings of God. Every blessing we receive from God has the same note joined to it. It says, "There's more to follow."
He chose us, but there's more to follow.
He called us, but there's more to follow.
He regenerated us, but there's more to follow.
He justified us, but there's more to follow.

He acquitted us, but there's more to follow.
He declared us righteous, but there's more to
follow.
He set us apart to Himself, but there's more to
follow.
He adopted us, but there's more to follow.
He gave us eternal life, but there's more to follow.
Why? Because, "God is rich in Mercy."

And that's the Gospel Truth!

Chapter 33

The Missing Element

Nowadays, there is an enormous missing element in many of those who say they have become Christians. The missing element is that, although these folk say that they are believers, they have never known or felt they ever were ruined sinners. They will admit they were or are sinners, but only generally so and when it comes right down to it they know nothing of the utter ruin that sin has made of them. They don't seem to have ever known any conviction of sin; yet, they say they have come to Jesus. However, when we examine what they mean by that, we usually find that they came to Jesus because they needed a provider, or an insurance policy that delivered from Hell, or a friend in times of need or whatever else they have been told Jesus is.

However, they do not, come to Jesus seeking Him as the only Saviour from sin. Why not? Because they have no real concept that their sin has totally ruined them (Isaiah 1:5). They have no actual idea that what they deserve is damnation and death (2 Thessalonians 1:8).

When a sinner first senses the conviction of sin, he smells trouble and begins to realize that he deserves wrath! He becomes aware that his whole past life has been a life without God and against God. Deep within him he begins to ask, *"What must I do to be saved?"* The more he knows of the reality and awfulness of his sin the more he asks questions like, *"Is it possible that my sin can actually be forgiven?* (Psalm 130:40). He is like the awakened revenue collector in scripture who cried out, "God, be a mercy seat to me a sinner"(Luke 18:13).

What about you? Have you turned to Jesus as your only hope? I didn't ask you if you have ever raised your hand during an altar call and prayed a little prayer asking Jesus into your heart. What I'm asking is, have you been pierced and ruined by your sins? Have you grasped that it is only by the shed blood of Christ that there is mercy for you? Have you understood that on your best day, even after trying diligently to serve the Lord, you deserve only death, doom and damnation? Have you grasped that, without the mercy and grace of God, you are finished?

Becoming a believer is much more than having a new, good feeling! In fact, it often starts with a very bad feeling---the feeling of dread! Your sins are awful; they have separated you from God (Isaiah 59:2)! There's an alarm that goes along with this! But, the good news is that the greatness of your sins is no barrier to your acceptance with God! Why's that? It's because God has provided a wrath offering for sins and for sinners, and that wrath offering is the Lord Jesus Christ Himself (Romans 3:25)! And it is this same Jesus who satisfied the holy wrath of God when he died as the sinner's substitute: and it is this same Jesus who is at this moment our Mercy Seat.

And that's the Gospel Truth!

Chapter 34:

The Gift of Repentance

According to scripture, repentance is a gift. Acts 5:3 says, *"Him (Christ) hath God exalted with His right hand to be a prince and saviour for to give repentance to Israel and forgiveness of sins."* What wonderful gifts God gives! He gives us repentance to come to Christ and continues to give us repentance as we grow and mature in Christ. In fact it is usually after we come to Christ that we find out what true repentance is. As Thomas Brooks, the Puritan, said,
"A true penitent must go on from faith to faith, from strength to strength; he must never stand still nor turn back. Repentance is a grace, and must have its daily operation as well as other graces. True repentance is a continued spring, where the waters of godly sorrow are always flowing: 'My sin is ever before me' (Psalm 51:3).
An old Irish woman once said to the minister, *"Pastor we didn't know what sin was until you came to this church."* Amusing! What she was trying to say was that it's only after we begin to grow in grace that we discover what sin really is.

Thank God for His gift of repentance! It always leads us to the Throne of Grace where we confess our sins to Jesus our faithful High Priest. If we have sinned, what's the point in killing ourselves with the guilt of our actions? We should plead guilty and throw ourselves on the mercy of the court.

Some people beat themselves over and over because of past failures. However, often times this is just another form of self-righteousness whereby they are saying to God, *"See Lord, see how sorry I really am. Take note of this and forgive me because I am really repenting here."* But how foolish it is to try to impress God with our repentance! Take everything to the blood! That's God's provision for our guilt.

"If we confess our sins He is faithful and just to forgive us our sins and to cleanse us from all unrighteousness" (1 John 1:9).

In the ancient world a criminal was sometimes compelled to be joined face-to- face with a dead body, and to carry it about until the horrible, decaying, stench of death destroyed the life of the living man.

Virgil, in his Aeneid, describes this cruel punishment with the following words:

"The living and the dead at his command
Were coupled face to face, and hand to hand;
Till choked with stench, in loathed embraces tied,
The lingering wretches pined away and died."

Without Christ, we are shackled to a dead corpse -- our sinfulness. But in grace, God gives us the gifts of repentance and faith to free us from the consequences of who we are. Through grace, the gift of repentance gives us a hatred of sin; it helps us to turn from sin and births a determination to, with the Lord's help, forsake it.

Repentance is a continual life-long act. It grows continually within us. Spurgeon said, "I believe the Christian on his death-bed will more bitterly repent than ever he did before. It is a thing to be done all your life long. Sinning and repenting— sinning and repenting make up a Christian's life. Repenting and believing in Jesus—repenting and believing in Jesus, make up the consummation of his happiness."

Repentance is a grace gift. Some people preach it as a condition of salvation. This is sheer legalistic nonsense! There are no conditions of salvation. But to those whom He saves, He gives the excellent and gracious gift of repentance.

And that's the Gospel Truth!

Chapter 35

Righteous Grace Part 1

God is the God of all Grace (1 Peter 5:10). He is also the God of righteousness (Ezra 9:15). It is as we see that God saves us, not only by grace, but also through righteousness that we enjoy His full and perfect peace (Isaiah 45:21, Romans 4:5; Isaiah 26:3).

At the heart of the gospel, we discover that grace is, as Horatius Bonar terms it, "Righteous Grace." Unless we understand this, we will continually struggle with assurance and peace. God justifies the ungodly (Romans 4:5) and does so as a matter, not solely of love, but also of righteousness. At the cross, the justice of God punished Christ as though He were the worst of sinners (2 Corinthians 5:21). Because God refused to gloss over the sin problem, Christ was condemned as though He were us. Justice has, therefore, been satisfied.

Luther, at first, struggled to understand this very thing. One day he read David's prayer in Psalm 71:2: "Save me in thy righteousness" and cried out, "What does this mean? I can understand how God can damn me in His righteousness, but if he would save me it must surely be in His mercy." Through time, however, He came to understand that gospel grace is indeed righteous grace.

In the Gospel, we are not confronted with a vague forgiveness, arising out of some sort of paternal love on the part of a bemused God. That would be far from righteous grace. We've got to get to grips with this! We need to know both the righteous and gracious basis of our acceptance before God. Indeed, if we are not clear on this, we have no gospel! If we take away either righteousness or grace from the gospel, we have eliminated its very life-blood, and there is, as Spurgeon says, *"Nothing left worth preaching, worth believing, or worth contending for."*

Righteous grace is at the heart and soul of the gospel: without it, the gospel is dead. Without righteous grace, there is no comfort for the troubled conscience. From first to last, everything in salvation is of grace and that grace comes to us righteously.

Additionally, to help us understand this we need to ask:

1) Did God recognize our absolute guilt, but chose to ignore it since He is our Father?
2) Or, did God acquit us because He loves us and, at the back of it all, He is very good-natured?
3) Or, is God indifferent to sin?
4) Or, was it that because God's absolute holiness demanded He took action against our sin, He punished Christ Jesus at the cross of Calvary?

So, how say you? On what basis does God acquit us? Are we declared not-guilty because God is kind and tender? Or, does God forgive us in a righteous, just and gracious manner? We must be clear on this. We must be clear that, at the cross, our sins were paid for by our substitute. Christ was legally cursed on our behalf (Galatians 3:13). Our gracious acquittal is, therefore, based on the work of righteousness. It was righteousness that had condemned us in the first place. It was righteousness that had barred us from heaven and if ever we were to be saved it had to be done righteously.

Now that Christ has been righteously punished in our place, our condemnation has been righteously and graciously removed (Romans 8:1). Christ has died in place of the ungodly and has been righteously condemned. Believers have now been declared righteous, not because the Lord is nice, but because of righteous grace. Christ died and intercepted our well-earned wrath as He purged and took our sin away (Romans 3:25, Hebrews 1:3, John 1:29).

Since the perfect righteousness of Christ has now been graciously reckoned to us, it would be, therefore, an unrighteous thing for God to condemn anyone for whom Christ died (Romans 4:22-25, Romans 8:34).

And that's the Gospel Truth!

Chapter 36

Righteous Grace: Part 2

It's one thing to feel good about the gospel, but quite a different matter to grasp its ramifications. I have met many professing Christians who, for example, are 'martyrs' to a bad conscience. They know the words, *"saved by grace,"* but suspect that grace means, 'God's lackadaisical kindness'. Not having understood that the grace which saves is righteous grace, they have no peace. The 'gospel' that they know ministers calm to neither their mind nor their conscience (Jeremiah 6:14).

For true peace we, as gospel believers, continually find ourselves going back to the cross. When your conscience tells you that you are a rat, then asks you if you are sure that God is merciful?" ... What do you do? And just as you are thinking about the question, your conscience pipes up again saying "What if God grows weary of you and forgets to be gracious?" What can you say? The only answer to these accusations is the cross for it boldly declares that, "Christ Jesus was set forth as a substitutionary wrath offering for sin." At the cross, we learn that He saves by both love and justice. At the cross, we learn that we are saved as a matter of righteousness grace (Romans 3:24-26).

He saves us justly. This is good news for we easily could imagine a scenario where God could cease to be merciful, but we could never envision Him ceasing to be just.

Righteous grace is no new concept. In the Old Testament, the blood of the sin offering was sprinkled on the mercy seat. Justice and mercy combined. The sinner was, consequently, saved, not only by grace, but also saved righteously. Likewise, in the New Covenant, the God of the gospel graciously justified the ungodly by ruthlessly punishing our sins in the person of our substitute Jesus Christ. Although we are saved by grace alone, saving grace is never alone for it is inseparably joined to righteousness. Our salvation and right standing with God now rest on the righteous and gracious work which God has already accomplished for us, outside of us, in the Person of Jesus Christ (Romans 3:24).

Two thousand years ago there was an objective, actual, historical event when God Himself broke into human history as one of us. He became our representative and was so identified with us that all which He did was, not only done for us, but was exactly the same as if we had done it ourselves. When He graciously bore the punishment for our sin, we were righteously punished in Him. When He arose, we arose. When He was exalted to the right hand of the majesty on high so were we (Ephesians 2:6)! It is finished! We can now be at peace.

Have you ever had a troubled conscience? I have! The following are some scriptures (*in personalized form*) that I have frequently used to defeat the accusations of a bad conscience. Take these wonderful truths and confess them.

"Christ died for my sins" (1 Corinthians 15:3).
"He was wounded for my transgressions; he was bruised for my iniquities" (Isaiah 53:5).
"Christ was once offered to bear my sins" (Hebrews 9:28).
Who gave himself for me, that he might redeem me (Titus 2:14).
He was "delivered for my offences and was raised for my justification" (Romans 4:25).
He "gave himself for my sins" (Galatians 1:4)

"Christ died for me" (Romans 5:6).

"He has appeared to put away my sin by the sacrifice of himself" (Hebrews 9:26).

See also 1 Peter 4:1, 1Peter 3:18, 1 Peter 2:24.

Notice how the words, *'Himself'* and *'He'* appear frequently in the preceding verses. This is because the gracious and righteous Lord Himself is our salvation. He is our robe of righteousness.

Someone once asked Irenaeus, the 2nd Century, iconic champion of the faith, "*Irenaeus, what has Christ brought that other religious leaders have not brought?*" He answered, "*He brought Himself.*"

That's what makes our gospel different. God came here Himself to righteously and gracious deal with sin and sinners. This is good news for the troubled conscience.

And that's the Gospel Truth!

Chapter 37

Righteous Grace Part 3

It is written, *"The soul that sins it shall die"* (Ezekiel 18:4). In the light of this scripture, we see that each one of us was under the death sentence. Indeed, the righteous demands of God made our death a necessity. Therefore, to meet this dreadful obligation and to rescue us, the Eternal One, in grace and love, became one of us and died in our place.

Let's say someone was to die for a person for whom there was no need to die; we would be unlikely to call this death a proof of affection. Quite the contrary, we would likely consider it a strange and illogical demonstration of pointlessness. However, to die for someone, when there was really a need for dying ... now that's the test of true and genuine love. The hymn writer said it well when he penned the lines,

"Here is love, vast as the ocean,
Loving-kindness as the flood,
When the Prince of Life, our Ransom,

Shed for us His precious blood.
Who His love will not remember?
Who can cease to sing His praise?
He can never be forgotten,
Throughout Heav'n's eternal days."

If ever we were to be saved from damnation, Christ Jesus had to die. Because of this necessity, grace and righteousness combined and led the eternal One to the cross. There at Calvary, He died in the sinner's place and thus made it a righteous thing for God to cancel the believing sinner's guilt and to rescind his sentence of death.

Thomas Watson, the Puritan, said, '*When we were rebelling—He was dying! When we had weapons in our hands—then He had the spear in His side! This is the very quintessence of love! "God demonstrates His own love for us in this: While we were still sinners, Christ died for us!" (Romans 5:8). When we were engulfed in misery and had lost our beauty—then Christ died for us. O amazing love, which should swallow up all our thoughts!"*

Had it not been for Christ's doing and dying, God and the sinner could not have met, and righteousness would have forbidden reconciliation. It was love working in harmony with righteous grace that secured our salvation.

"On the mount of crucifixion,
Fountains opened deep and wide;
Through the floodgates of God's mercy
Flowed a vast and gracious tide.
Grace and love, like mighty rivers,
Poured incessant from above,
And Heav'n's peace and perfect justice
Kissed a guilty world in love."

Unless God had punished our substitute at the cross, it would not have been correct for God to receive us or indeed, safe for us to come to Him. But now, in Christ, mercy and truth have met together, righteousness and peace have kissed (Psalm 85:10). Now, through Christ, gracious salvation is also righteous. It is as faith grasps both the righteous and gracious nature of the work of Calvary that our conscience finds peace (Hebrews 9:14). Peace flows to us as we see that our reconciliation is anchored in the righteousness of God (Ephesians 2:13-16) and this righteous reconciliation will stand every test and will last throughout eternity.

The troubled conscience can only find true peace in the gospel as it understands that Christ died for the ungodly (Romans 5:6). Faith grasps that God justifies, not the godly, but the ungodly (Romans 4:5). The righteous grace which is ours, through the sin-bearing work of Christ, tells us that there can be no possible condemnation nor even a hint of mild disapproval for one who is saved by the free grace of God alone (Romans 8:1). God is Just, yet the Justifier of the ungodly (Romans 3:26)! This is astonishing news! This is super abounding grace!

And that's the Gospel Truth!

Chapter 38

Misunderstood Matters about Grace Part 1

The meaning of grace is quite often misunderstood. It is sometimes presented as a soft spot for sinners in the heart of God, or as some kind of benevolence on behalf of the Almighty that disregards the sin question. This is entirely incorrect! As we have already seen, grace, Bible grace, loving grace, is righteous grace. Saving grace never bypasses the cross!

Because of the cross we learn that God saves, not because He has an easy-going inbuilt compassion, but saves, rather, by having dealt ruthlessly with our sins when He laid them on Christ. Yes indeed, we are saved by grace, but it is righteous grace for it comes from the God who refused to ignore the awfulness of our sin. Our sin was not swept under the carpet; rather, God publicly placarded His Son and set Him forth as a wrath offering for sin on our behalf (Romans 3:25-26). Grace is, therefore, both free and costly; it's free to us, but it has been so very costly to Him!

Another misunderstood thing about grace is that we often feel as though we have to seek it. God's grace, however, does not wait for us to seek it out, but rather it comes seeking us. Jesus made this clear when He declared that He had come to seek and to save that which was lost (Luke 19:10). So wonderful and excellent is His grace that He sought us out before we even knew we were lost! This is why we sing of His grace as being 'Amazing'. We were really and truly lost, but He really and truly came looking for us and found us!

Even now, after being saved for many years, grace continues to come and seek us out. We still have tendencies to stray and wander off. As the Hymn writer said,

Prone to wander, Lord I feel it
Prone to leave the God I love,
Take my heart Lord, take and seal it,
Seal it for thy courts above.

I once heard about an old deacon who always prayed, *"Lord, prop us up on our leanin' side..."* Someone asked him why he prayed that prayer so frequently and fervently. He answered, *'Well sir, you see, it's like this... I got an old barn out back. It's been there a long time, it's withstood a lot of weather, it's gone through a lot of storms, and it's stood for many years. It's still standing. But one day I noticed it was leaning to one side a bit. So I went and got some pine poles and propped it up on its leaning side so it wouldn't fall. Then I got to thinking about that and how much I was like that old barn. Sometimes I find myself leaning to one side from time to time, so I like to ask the Lord to prop us up on our leaning side, 'cause I figure a lot of us get to leaning, at times."*

I like that, but do know what? I'm worse than that for, at times, I find myself, not just leaning over on one side, but leaning over on every side and ready to collapse. Have you ever been that way? If you have, here's the good news ... grace does not wait for us to cry out for help; grace is already there seeking to restore and strengthen us before we ever begin leaning. Grace goes to work and brings us back to our merciful High priest whose throne is a throne of grace and who delights to give us grace to help in the time of need (Hebrews 4:16).

And that's the Gospel Truth!

Chapter 39

Misunderstood Matters about Grace Part 2

Another thing about grace is that it is completely undeserved! I question if we really understand this. I suspect that many of us pay lip service to the undeserved nature of grace, but often the power of this truth has not permeated the depths of our being.

If we don't believe that grace is entirely undeserved, we should consider how utterly worthless we were when grace first saved us. We were enemies of God and without strength (Romans 5:6, 5:10). We were as John McNeill graphically put it, "Ownerless dogs prowling the garbage heaps of humanity." Now ask yourself this; have you through the years become so wonderful that you are now worth saving? I hope you answer no! The truth is that grace saves people who have absolutely, *"no good thing"* in them worth saving (Romans 7:18). If we think there is one good thing about us ... one shred of perfect, unadulterated goodness that deserves to be saved, there is no room for grace.

If we believe in salvation by grace alone, we have recognized that we are, in ourselves, destitute of everything. We are in agreement with the scripture when it says, *"the whole head is sick, and the whole heart faint"* (Isaiah 1:5). Believing this, we have no difficulty accepting that grace both sent the gospel to us, and opened our eyes to it.

Grace is both the seeker and the finder. It was the personification of grace who sought and found Zacchaeus in Luke 19. It was grace that found Noah and by grace that Noah was saved (Genesis 6:8). Indeed, the sole reason that any of us love the Lord is because of grace and grace alone.

If God withdrew His gracious hand from us, then we would be exposed, naked and undone before the awful holiness of God. But grace saves those who cannot, by their own efforts, produce one continuing trace of goodness or even one suggestion of holiness that could recommend them to Heaven. This is good news for people like me! Grace is for the lost, the guilty and the hopeless. Grace is for those who were too weak to walk towards God, but who were abundantly energetic when it came to running away from Him. These are the only people whom grace saves!

By the way, in this day and age when absolute right and wrong have been almost entirely dispensed with, it is, humanly speaking, very difficult to get people saved since so few will admit that they are actually lost, incurably lost and entirely dependent on someone else to save them Why, after all, consent to someone else saving you when you don't know you need to be saved in the first place? When it comes to evangelism, we can get people to raise their hands at the end of a meeting because they want to go to heaven, but let's face it, who in their right mind wants to go to hell? This kind of 'soul winning' activity can often be a long way off from bringing salvation! Salvation is for lost people, for ruined sinners and for hopeless cases. Salvation is only for those who need grace.

The Lord gives us grace upon grace (John 1:16; James 4:6). In other words, we both start and continue this Christian life by grace alone. Grace is the great changer of lives and the subduer of indwelling sin. A man may spend his entire life trying to reform, but we are saved from beginning to end by grace, pure grace, righteous grace and that alone. John Newton, the author of the grand old hymn, "Amazing Grace", said it like this,

"By various maxims, forms and rules-
That pass for wisdom in our schools-
I sought my passions to restrain,
But all my efforts proved in vain.

But since my Savior I have known
Are all my rules reduced to one-
To keep my Lord by faith in view-
This faith supplies, and motive too."

And that's the Gospel Truth!

Chapter 40

Misunderstood Matters about Grace Part 3

When it comes to salvation, another misunderstood thing about grace is assuming that our faith creates the grace of God. However, the truth is that grace, righteous grace, already lived in the heart of God before anyone ever exercised faith. In our un-saved state, we were excluded from the life of God and lived in the lusts of the flesh, fulfilling the desires of the flesh and the mind (Ephesians 2:1-4). But God graciously made us alive unto Himself (Ephesians 2:5). Faith came because of grace. In fact, faith is nowhere, in the scriptures, said to create grace; it's quite the opposite. Our faith does not make God gracious. God's righteous grace already existed before faith was given. For by grace you are saved (Ephesians 2:5).

Because of grace we are given faith. Faith will cause us to grasp that the sacrifice of Christ at

Calvary is a righteous, finished sacrifice (John 19:30). As believers, faith continues to lead us to hug the truth that, in Christ crucified, righteousness and grace have already embraced and we are now covered, not merely by grace, but with the robe of righteousness.

When faith reads, *"I will greatly rejoice in the LORD, my soul shall be joyful in my God; for he hath clothed me with the garments of salvation, he hath covered me with the robe of righteousness,* (Isaiah 61:10) it says a vigorous amen! Faith sees that the reason God loved us and took delight in us was not discovered in some goodness or worth within us but found, rather, in the gracious good-pleasure of God Himself (Matthew 12:32). Faith sees that Christ's destiny is our destiny. Faith sees that He was made alive and that we were made alive together with him. Faith believes that He was raised up and that we were raised up together with him. Faith reckons that He was made to sit at the right hand of the Father in heavenly places, and we have been made to sit together with him. Why? There is one answer and only one. It's grace, pure grace, sovereign grace (Ephesians 2:5-7).

So let's say it again, faith does not bring grace into existence. If we have received grace, then it not because we gave anything to deserve it … and that includes faith! Let's face it, if we believe that our faith brought grace into existence then we must conclude that we are co-providers of salvation. Perish the thought!

God saves us by his grace, and not because of our faith! Although we were dead in our sins (Ephesians 2:1), "God, who is rich in mercy, because of the great love with which he loved us, even when we were dead in our trespasses, quickened (made us alive) together with Christ — by grace you have been saved" (Ephesians 2:4-5).

Nonetheless, someone objects saying, "But, we need faith." I reply, "Of course we do; we are not suggesting that faith is not vital, but nowhere does God look and see if we have faith before He justifies us. We are saved "through" faith and not because of it (Ephesians 2:7). Faith is the instrument, the channel through which we receive salvation. Grace, on the other hand, is the very ground of our salvation.

We are dependent on Him, and not on our faith. He is completely reliable, He never fails. Our faith, on the other hand, often fails but the object of our faith, the Lord Jesus, never!

Faith receives salvation, but it is a very poor foundation on which to attempt to build our salvation. We build on Christ alone + nothing!

This God is the God we adore,
Our faithful, unchangeable Friend,
Whose love is as great as His power,
And knows neither measure nor end!
'Tis Jesus, the First and the Last,
Whose Spirit shall guide us safe home;
We'll praise Him for all that is past,
And trust Him for all that's to come.

And that's the Gospel Truth!

Chapter 41

He Saves Even the Worst of Us!

I never cease to be amazed at the sovereign hand of God in bringing His lost sheep into the fold. Have you ever heard the story of the conversion of William P Mackay? It's a wonderful illustration of how the Lord, in His greatness, saves even the worst of people.

William P. Mackay was born, in Scotland, in the year 1839. At the age of 17, he left for college. However, his mother, a godly Christian woman, didn't want him to go. She feared that he was heading down a path of destruction. Nevertheless, she turned him over to the Lord, and let him go on his way.

Before his departure, she gave him a Bible to take with him, and in the fly-leaf of the Bible, she wrote his name, her name and a Bible verse. Mackay left for college and then went on to the university medical school, but he fell in with a bad lot and became an expert at godless living. Then one day, in a drunken spree, he pawned the Bible to get money for more drink.

Mackay had gone completely off the rails. His life was now filled with dissolute living. Yet, at the same time, the young Scotsman went on to become a very successful doctor, eventually becoming the head of the largest hospital in Edinburgh. Forsaking his upbringing, he became a committed atheist, and was even elected president of a society of atheists in the city.

One day, an accident victim was admitted to the hospital and was placed under Dr Mackay's direct care. The patient, learning that he only had a few hours to live, asked Dr Mackay, "Will you please send for my landlady, and ask her to bring me the Book?" The doctor agreed, and shortly thereafter the landlady arrived with "The Book."
Within a short time, the patient died. Dr Mackay was curious as to what kind of book the patient had wanted. He asked the nurse, "What about the book that he asked for?" Was it is his bank book or date book?" The nurse replied, "No, it was neither of those. It is still under his pillow, see for

yourself." The doctor reached under the pillow and pulled out "The Book"... it was the Bible. It looked familiar and when he opened it, his eyes fell immediately upon the front flyleaf. To his amazement ... it was the very Bible he had received from his mother, the one that he had pawned years before. He saw his name, his mother's name and the Bible verse she inscribed ... John 3:16.

Mackay was overwhelmed. He slipped the Bible under his coat and rushed back to his private office. Once inside his office, he fell to his knees and prayed that God would have mercy on him, and save him.
Dr Mackay immediately contacted his mother to tell her of his salvation, and how God used the Bible she gave him to dramatically answer her prayers.

By the grace of God, William Patton Mackay, the world renowned doctor went on to become a world renowned Presbyterian preacher, well-known author and songwriter. In fact, it was from his pen that we received the excellent hymn:

We praise Thee o God,

For the Son of thy love,
For Jesus who has died
And is now gone above
"Hallelujah, Thine the glory.
Hallelujah, Amen.
Hallelujah, Thine the glory.
Revive us again!"

Here is a sample of his preaching,

"Jesus did all the saving work. He brought the cross to our level. We get saved by looking to Him... Lie down as a wounded, helpless, ungodly sinner and look away from yourself to Jesus..."

I hope this brief word encourages us to stay resolute in prayer for our loved ones. The Lord's hand cannot be stopped. He can and does save the worst of people.

And that's the Gospel Truth!

Chapter 42

When Necessary Use Words ...?

Francis of Assisi has been attributed with the quote, "Preach the gospel always and when necessary use words." Whether or not he actually said this is a matter of inconsequence. What matters is that this anti - gospel statement is often heralded by 'enlightened' evangelicals, so called, to justify their lack of evangelistic endeavour. They maintain that all we have to do is to live out the Christian life. If we do this, they insist, people will notice how god-like we are and will then convert to Christ.

When it comes to this subject, urban legends abound. The heretic, Charles Finney, who in spite of his distorted and twisted denial of the doctrine of forensic Justification is still popular in many quarters, was supposedly so holy that one day, he walked into a factory and just stood there.

According to this fable, what happened next was that every worker in the factory came under conviction of sin, stopped working and cried out for mercy.

"Well," you say, "don't you believe that story?"
Not a bit of me!
"Well why not?" you ask.
I'll tell you why not. I don't believe it, because it's not true.
"But how do you know it's not true?"
I know it's not true for the simple reason, that when weighed by and measured against the gospel it turns out to be false.

Let me explain. Where, for example, do we read in the gospels that Christ walked into places and, just by standing there, converted all the people? Yet, Christ Jesus was pure, holy and sinless. He was God manifest in the flesh. It doesn't get purer than that! However, His purity and holiness converted no one in the imaginary Finney manner.

Also, Jesus grew up in a home where His brothers and sisters did not believe in Him. His spotless, holy life, evidently, did nothing to move the unbelievers in His family towards salvation. In fact, there is no evidence that His brothers James and Jude got converted until after the resurrection. So much for the theory that our good, good lives will be the source of converting people.

Now, lest I am misunderstood, I of course believe that we should aim, by the gracious power of the Spirit, to lead lives worthy of the gospel. Our lives should bring glory to the Father (Matthew 5:16), should become sound doctrine (Titus 2:1); should be such that no evil thing can be spoken of us (Titus 2:7-8); and should adorn the doctrine of God (Titus 2:10), but, God forbid that we should think that this is the way to get people saved.

For people to get saved, the gospel must be told. In spite of what St. Francis, or whomever it was that said it, words are always necessary. The use of words is the New Testament pattern.

Consider the following scriptures:

Acts 8:25: And they, when they had testified and preached the word of the Lord, returned to Jerusalem, and preached the gospel in many villages of the Samaritans.

Acts 15:7: --- God made choice among us, that the Gentiles by my mouth should hear the word of the gospel, and believe.

Ephesians 1:13: In whom ye also trusted, after that ye heard the word of truth, the gospel of your salvation;

Colossians 1:5: For the hope which is laid up for you in heaven, whereof ye heard before in the word of the truth of the gospel;

Hebrews 4:2: For unto us was the gospel preached, as well as unto them;

1 Peter 1:25: .. And this is the word which by the gospel is preached unto you.

Words are necessary for the gospel, because the gospel is a past historical event. We can't live in a way that effectively communicates events of history. We, of course, can reflect the benefits of the gospel in our life style, but this is not the same as actually preaching the gospel. Besides that, the gospel is not about our experience. It's about the unique, never to be repeated, experience of the God/Man and with all due apologies to St. Francis, or whomever, it is impossible, therefore, to declare it without words.

And that's the Gospel Truth!

Conclusion

Jesus is the Good News! He is the sum and substance of the gospel! But what does that mean in everyday life? One of the dangers that we face is that we may well know the wonderful facts of the gospel, but do not know how they are intended to interpret our lifestyle? In other words, are we not gospel driven in our attitude and approach to life?

To be gospel driven, we need to know the entire gospel and its applications. In doing so, we will not permanently camp on any one part of the gospel to the exclusion of the others. In the gospel, for example, we are presented with Christ's incarnation and impeccable life. These are essential gospel truths to embrace, but we dare not stop there and make these facts the entirety of our gospel. The gospel is much more!
By the way, if the gospel stopped with the incarnation and sinless life of Christ, then no one would ever have been saved! That God came to earth as a genuine, sinless human is a precious and powerful gospel truth, but it is not the entirety of

the good news! The incarnation in and of itself saves no one! The incarnation is the beginning of the good news; it is as Bonar says, the Alpha, but not the Omega. The gospel in its fullness tells us much more. It tells us of the active and passive obedience of Christ, of how He both lived and died as our substitute and Federal Head (Romans 5:12-21).

Indeed, the Christ event is the centre of the Bible, and at its heart we discover the cross of Christ. The cross has lain from eternity in the very heart of God (Revelation 13:8). It was no afterthought. Indeed, before there ever was a sinner on earth, there was a Saviour in heaven.

For a full gospel, therefore, we must have the entire gospel! However, simple as the constituent parts of the gospel are, we must not stop with them for there is even more to the gospel than these simple bare facts of history. For example, the gospel presents us with the person of Christ. It proclaims that, this person is the perfect demonstration of God. If we have seen Him, we have seen the Father (John 14:9). Look closely at the cross. It is there, amidst the gore, that we see His glory. Jesus prophesied this saying, "When you have lifted up the Son of man then you will know that I am" (John 8:28). The cross, therefore, shows not only the greatness, wisdom, grace and justice of God but also reveals God Himself.

This crucified Christ died, was buried, rose again, ascended to heaven and now sits in exalted authority as our, "Advocate with the Father," (1 John 2:1). "He ever lives to make intercession for us" (Hebrews 7:25). He is our perfect Prophet, Priest and King. He is the Lamb, the Lion, the Way, the Door and everything behind the door. He is Grace, Justice, Mercy and Holiness, the Friend of sinners and the Hater of sin. He is the Life, the Light, the Resurrection, our Destiny and the one who will, on that day, consummate everything that He inaugurated when He physically and visibly returns for His blood bought people (Hebrews 9:28).

These are some of the astounding facts of the gospel. It is no wonder then that the gospel is the central message of the apostolic, New Testament Church. We, as gospel driven believers knows this! The person, work and offices of the Lord Jesus are that on which we rest our entire confidence.

Now, as gospel driven believers, we seek to know and live in the applications of the gospel. We grasp, for example, that Jesus not only came and lived for us but that He also came and lived as us! He not only died and rose for us, He also died and rose as us. When He ascended, we ascended. When He received the approval and welcome of the Father we received it also! He is our man in Heaven. He is our representative. He has done everything as though we had done it ourselves. This means that, at this very minute, if you are a believer, found in Christ, God is thrilled with you! Do you believe that? Do you agree with that? At this very moment, you are accepted in the Beloved One! But you say, *"This cannot be true for I am such a failure as a follower of Christ."* That may well be the case; you may indeed be the hugest disappointment you have ever met! But in the light of that, there is no better time to preach and apply the gospel to your situation!

The issue with the Father today is not you; the issue with the Father is the Lord Jesus Christ. You are not the centre of all things, Christ Jesus is! It is the Father's verdict of Christ that is of central importance! And what is the Father's verdict? His verdict of Christ is, *"This is my beloved son in whom I am well pleased"* (Matthew 3:17). That is why, at this very moment, we are, "Accepted in the Beloved," the Lord Jesus! You may be dejected, distressed and depressed when you look at yourself, but preach the gospel to yourself and apply it. Speak to yourself. Say things like,

"Arise, my soul, arise; shake off thy guilty fears;
The bleeding sacrifice in my behalf appears:
Before the throne my surety stands,
My name is written on His hands."
On account of the finished work, we have a high
Priest in Heaven. God, consequently, does not see
our sins. He does not count them against us. What
does God see? He sees our priest, His perfect Son,
His perfect sacrifice and perfect blood! He sees
Christ's entire perfections and is more than
satisfied with Him.
Yes indeed, God wants us to confess our sins, but
we are not to make them the focus of our life.
Instead, He desires that we focus on Christ and
enjoy Him! By doing so, we have the surest way to
grow in grace.
And that's the Gospel Truth!

The End

Please tell others about this book (it is also available as an eBook/Kindle at Amazon.com or Amazon.co.uk).

If you have been helped by this material, please give this publication a review on Amazon.

For more of Miles McKee's writings visit www.milesmckee.com/books

Other titles by Miles McKee include,

Smooth Stones to Slay Goliath

Getting into Heaven before they Close the Door.

Jesus is God ... Always was and always will be: Part 1

Jesus is God ... Always was and always will be: Part 2

Jesus is God ... Always was and always will be: Part 3

The Gospel Truth about Jesus

The Gospel Truth about the Blood

Many of the chapters of, "And that's the Gospel Truth" first appeared in the Wednesday Word. To subscribe, for free, to the Wednesday Word, email miles@milesmckee.com with the word 'Subscribe' in the subject line.

Made in the USA
Columbia, SC
11 April 2018